TWO TO
GET READY

TWO TO GET READY

by

Henry V. Sattler, C.SS.R.

Fides Publishers, Inc.

Notre Dame, Indiana

173
S253

To
EUGENE — LORETTA — HENRY

TABLE OF CONTENTS

Chapter One

LOOKING FORWARD

TWO TO GET READY

The medical profession is a captivating one. The "Man in White" with searching eyes and skillful hands, rushing on his errands of mercy to men, is the theme of many a story and TV program. This is so true that the "pitchmen" in the TV advertisements, for everything from tooth paste to pills, are often dressed in white to give the aura of professional medical approval to what they are trying to sell.

This respect for medicine is truly deserved. When a boy decides to become a doctor, he enters on a tremendous gamble. I doubt whether one boy in fifty who would like to be a doctor ever achieves his goal. Though the medical profession is crying for more doctors, the requirements grow stricter and the training more difficult each year. A candidate is screened not only for intelligence and skill but for personality and motivation. Even his external deportment is checked and corrected. Then he spends long years of training in theory and laboratory work before he is even allowed to walk through a hospital ward to so much as look at a patient under supervision. When he finally is awarded the diploma and can demand to be called "Doctor," he still must intern for at least a year under stern supervision.

None of us think this instruction is too long or too hard. We wouldn't trust our lives to anyone trained less extensively. Some of us won't even go to a doctor less well-trained than a specialist, who spends three to five years longer in training than our regular M.D.

The same is true in lesser things. No one lets a contract to a builder who only knows how to dig a ditch. No one gets his house wired by a man who can only change a light plug. No one calls a plumber, a lawyer, an accountant, or even watches an actor or actress who has not had extensive preparation and training.

But there is a "profession" even more prominent in the imagination of the American people than that of the doctor, lawyer, politician, or actor. Watch any TV show; read any newspaper, magazine, or book; listen to almost any conversation and you will find that *love, marriage,* and *family life* are more in the thoughts of American people than any other topic. Yet, we seem to think that all it takes to accomplish happiness in marriage is a man, a woman, two dollars, and a marriage license!

Who prepares for marriage? What man asks himself whether his choice of work, or play, or food, or education will help him make a good husband and father? What young woman asks herself whether her homework, her conversation, her hobbies, her skills will make her a good wife and mother? What boy or girl demands requirements of personality, training, and skill before taking the other "for better or for worse"? A girl who wouldn't dream of allowing a friend to give her even a home permanent without beauty training will blissfully marry a man who has not yet demonstrated his ability to earn a living for himself, much less for a family. A young man will marry his "dream girl" almost on sight without testing his dream to see whether it should not be classified as a nightmare!

Not only are young people neglecting to prepare for marriage, they don't even know what it is. Suppose a budding young doctor did not know that medicine and biological science were to be used in his profession—how could he choose his school or his courses? Suppose someone wanted to be a plumber and didn't know that pipes were to be installed in the type of work he wanted to do! These examples are not as ridiculous as they sound. People want to get married. They know that they want to be united as man and woman, but they don't know what a man or a woman is. How can they put two beings together unless they know the differences? Usually men and woman are surprised and disappointed to find the other sex so different.

Some will say that it is easy to marry; all one needs is love. But what is love? Are you prepared to be able to love? A child loves ice cream or a toy. Could you safely marry on this kind of love? A teenager thrills to her favorite singer. Would this kind of thrill give a solid basis to living together for a lifetime? What kind of love is needed for marriage? And how do we explain the love in so many unions that doesn't seem to help husbands and wives to stay married?

Young people must prepare for marriage and parenthood. Boys must learn from an early age how to grow from boyhood into manhood—and into husbands and fathers. Girls must learn how to grow from childhood into womanhood and motherhood. If sex is the quality of being masculine or feminine, and masculinity and femininity are most completely developed in paternity and maternity, then sex education consists in training a boy to become a father and a girl to become a mother. Even those who remain celibate must prepare themselves in this way, since although they must sacrifice this noble way of life, they must respect and love it, and since they are going to work with people to whom marriage and family life are the supreme vocation.

Every young man and woman should prepare to love and to be loved, and to recognize love when it comes. Every boy and girl should have at least a basic understanding of the differences between a man and a woman. Every young person should know what marriage is and what it is for. When they have learned this, they should polish up their knowledge, skills, personalities, and motivations, so that when called into the lifetime of achievement which is marriage and family life, they can live up to their task with at least a minimum of competence. It takes "two to get ready" to make marriage go!

"Let those who are about to enter into married life, approach that state well disposed and well prepared . . ." (Pope Pius XI).

LOVE AND ROMANCE

For Americans, marriage is the most romantic of institutions. At least, our movies, songs, and novels would certainly make a stranger think so. Romantic emotion is the theme of most of them. The whole idea is illustrated in the story of two married women returning together from an afternoon movie. One turned to the other and sighed, "Oh, how I wish our husbands were with us this afternoon. Perhaps a little of that Gregory Peck would have rubbed off on them."

Though teenage girls seem to have a bit of priority on the swooning and sighs, no woman is without a desire for an emotional love affair to start off her marriage, and she is right. Romantic love should not by any means be despised. Even young men who are so uncomfortable when they are emotionally in love can and should look for romance before and in marriage.

The emotion of love is a rich and rewarding experience. It is something that changes the whole world. Truly does it give the lover rose-tinted glasses. To the romantic lover, sunny days are glittering experiences and gloomy days become incandescent. Colors are fluorescent; walking is floating; work is play; and sacrifices are but opportunities to prove love. And the whole world smiles approvingly, for all the world loves a lover. If the smiles sometimes seems cynical and disapproving, if the smilers sometimes turn to banter or even unmerciful teasing, it is not that people don't believe in romantic love, it is because they are envious of what they no longer have, or are unconsciously bitter that they have not experienced it. The young couple, for their part, though they may protest shyly to each other, "Don't throw bouquets at me," soon will proudly cry: "Let people say we're in love!"

So, by all means, look for romantic love and let it be like the match and the tinder which starts the quiet fire of deep love you hope to build together. But let your head guide your emotions. Be sure that you are not just in love with love, and that romance is not blinding you and leading you into a lifetime of sorrow. For, like the emotion of anger or fear, the emotion of love can lead you into difficulties unless you keep tight hold on the reins. Young people, so anxious to be in love, allow their desire for love to substitute for the real thing.

And future husbands, it is not enough for you to show your romantic love only while the chase is on! So many men go into marriage and say in action, if not in word, "I have paid you the supreme compliment of asking you to be my wife. Now be satisfied. Don't ask me to express love. Of course, I love you, what do you think I married you for?" For you, romance should not only be something that begins a courtship, but something that continues in marriage.

Yet, however wonderful romance is, it is not enough to build a marriage on. It is the delightful surrounding of a beautifully-served meal, but it is not the meal itself. And when the romance seems to fade, what then? "But romance can't fade for us!" you cry. Not only can it fade, but it must fade, or at least change, in order for real love to be built. Romance is what makes love easy, but when it is easy, is it the partner you love, or is it the fun of loving that you enjoy? God always takes the ecstasy away from time to time to test your love. He takes the zest out of praying at times to see whether we will continue because we love Him, or stop because we love merely the consolations of prayer. He takes the adventure out of the life of a priest or nun at times to see whether they love Him or the adventure of their dedication.

The disaster of building a marriage on romantic love alone is well-illustrated by the fact that one realistic minister of religion proposed that the Protestant ritual should be changed so that the minister should no longer say, "I join you in marriage so long as you both shall *live*," but "I join you in marriage so long as you both shall *love!*" In this way when the romantic love fades, the contract ceases to bind.

Yet, romantic love can't see that it will not last. Are there any love songs which say, "Let's fall in love for three years"? No, but we have the undying pledges of "Till the End of Time" and "Forever and Ever." However, our own experience tells us that all the thrills fade or at least change. If they do, then romantic love points to a deeper and more permanent love upon which to build marriage and family life.

So, young lovers, embrace your romance. Nurture it. Keep it flaming as long as you can, but don't marry for romance alone.

SEX AND SELFISHNESS

Our modern world is a sex-mad world. It looks toward sexual pleasure to bind up all its wounds. Our age is bounded by Freud and Kinsey on the "scientific" level; by D. H. Lawrence and Mickey Spillane in literature; by Clara Bow and Marilyn Monroe in entertainment.

Many young people, particularly young men, marry merely to find a legitimate outlet for their sexual drives. Consciously or unconsciously, with their appetites teased by suggestive books, "stag" magazines, salacious scenes and conversations, this is often their reason for marrying. For such people marriage is simply the state in which the

greatest amount and variety of sexual experience is to
be had.

Despite the fact that this approach, taken alone, is dangerous, it should be no secret that sexual love is the basis
of marriage and is naturally anticipated by the young
couple entering marriage. Church law defines marriage
consent in terms of the marriage union. "Matrimonial
consent is an act of will by which each party gives and
receives the perpetual and exclusive right to the body [of
the other] for actions adapted by nature to the generation
of progeny." (C. 1081, Par. 2). Both parties in an engagement should look forward to this sexual union with true
Christian joy. God Himself is the Author and Designer
of this pleasure and joy. It should be gratefully accepted.
To do otherwise would be to reject the gift of God and,
since God is the Giver, to reject Him.

Anticipation of this physical pleasure might not be in
the forefront of the bride's mind, but it could be very
much (and naturally so) in the mind of the groom.

The young man preparing for marriage, then, must always see clearly that it is the loving meaningfulness of
the marriage embrace which his future wife chiefly anticipates. She, or her side, must understand that her future husband will be more eagerly anticipating the physical act itself. Since it will be the loving duty of each to
meet the need of the other, this mutual awareness should
come easily. Love-making should not be a pleasure-taking
but a language which expresses love in action—one to
which God has attached an intense and holy pleasure.
Indeed, St. Thomas indicates that the fall of man de-
stroyed some of the intensity of this pleasure.

Yet, it is not enough to think of physical pleasure and
love, for both are implicitly directed towards the begetting of children. If in your deepest heart you are rejecting physical love and the children it ordinarily brings,
then please, for God's sake, for your own future happiness, for the real love you bear for your future partner,

postpone your marriage until you have your ideas matured. Better this than to marry now and discover later that you were not ready for anything more than mere companionship, security, or romance.

Granted that marriage is founded upon bodily union, physical love is by no means the be-all and the end-all of marriage. If a man (or woman) enters marriage only for the physical ecstasy, he will be doomed to bitter disappointment. There is a law of diminishing returns for this, as for any other, pleasure. It is a policy of confectionery owners to allow their sales girls to eat all the candy and ice cream they wish. The manager knows that soon there will be little or no desire for the sweets, once his employees have had their fill.

Mere physical desire, besides being doomed to inevitable disappointment, is basically self-seeking. Self-seeking can quickly turn to sheer selfishness in which the partner becomes merely an object which satisfies. A spouse used as a mere object—a thing—is rejected completely and can only come to hate the enslavement and the enslaver.

This is the story of the Casanovas and all the so-called "great lovers." They apparently loved only themselves and their own lust. They sought to obtain the maximum amount of personal pleasure. Since they soon tired of the same partner, their lives are strewn with the wreckage of one union after another, reflecting the pursuit of an ever-escaping satiety. These "great lovers" do not love, and inspire only disgust and hatred. Truly has a great psychiatrist said, "A marriage based only on physical attraction is doomed to failure from its inception."

SKILLS AND WILLS

Someone has described marriage as "giving up half of one's food to have the other half cooked." In these days of canned and frozen foods that is quite a presumption! Many young fellows are mistaken when they think that they are going to bring home the bacon and have it cooked, for many girls expect to learn in marriage itself the skills they need for it. One teenager asked by her mother how she expected to become a homemaker if she didn't learn now, answered, "Haven't you heard of in-service training?"

On the other hand, many girls get married because they get tired of working. They want to "stop working and marry." If this is what they are truly seeking, they become quickly disillusioned. For a young wife and mother, work is something she really only begins to do in marriage. But then there is a world of difference between "working for a living" and "living in work." Working for a living merely produces the money for keeping body and soul together. Living in work is satisfactory accomplishment.

It is true that successful marriage involves a convenient division of labor, in which two people accomplish a great deal more together than they could separately. Though it may not be true that two can live as cheaply as one, they certainly can live more efficiently than one. If a man had to do his own washing, cooking, cleaning, child care, shopping, etc., as well as earning a living, and if a woman had to do her own earning and investing, besides all the things usually expected of her in marriage, life would be more complex for both husband and wife. When both husband and wife attempt or are forced by circumstances to work outside the home, they soon find out how weary and complicated their lives become.

Then if marriage provides an agreeable division of labor in and out of the home, the first question an engaged person should ask is, "Am I able and willing to accept and carry out my kind of contribution to family life as husband and father, or as wife and mother?" The second question should be, "Is my future husband or wife able and willing to carry out his or her share?"

Every young woman looking forward towards marriage should develop and enjoy the skills of homemaking and child care. Creative cooking, tasteful home decorating, the ability to sew, the enthusiastic willingness to help a child to grow through all the stages of development, should be marks of the desirable young bride. After all, it takes a greater variety of true talents to be a culinary artist, interior decorator, clothing designer, landscape gardener, first-aid nurse, teacher, religious instructor, family judge, counselor, consoler, guidance director, source of courage to the family, and helpmate than it does to be any one of these things full-time while hiring someone else to do the others.

Every man anxious to marry should be able not only to support a wife and family (or at least have a *good* potential of doing so), but he should be willing and anxious to be the leader in his home, to relate that home to the community, to be the disciplinarian (which means to make disciples, followers!), to show an active, directive interest in every development in his home and family. His home will be his castle, where every act and need will be met by his loving concern, and not merely his hotel where he eats, sleeps, and re-creates his energy for a new day in the business world. His home-life is and must be a living—not a mere center from which he goes out to live in his business and recreational life.

To many people, perhaps to most, work is not a challenge which, when met and accomplished, satisfies and completes, but a necessary evil. They may talk of pleasant surroundings or the good friends they have at work, but not of the satisfying nature of the work itself. No married couple can build a good marriage on surroundings or personal attractiveness alone. They must picture with delight the achievements they anticipate by their division of labor. If they cannot enjoy family work, they should not marry. I am not saying that a wife should thrill to a scrub bucket or to a steam iron. I am not saying that a husband should swing his sledge with the same pleasure he swings his golf club or enjoy carrying storm windows as he would enjoy carrying a canoe on a fishing expedition. But a wife should be able to feel the satisfaction of a glistening floor and a snowy pile of clothes. A husband should glow with the accomplishment of his contribution to a new roof or a snug little house.

All this seems very prosaic as a preparation for marriage. Indeed, this division of labor and satisfaction in accomplishment is not enough to get married on. After all, the parts of the contract could possibly be "let out" to subcontractors, or similar working arrangements could be designed outside of marriage between several men or several women, or even groups of people. But contentment in this division of labor does provide one of the foundations of a happy, productive marriage union, and each engaged couple should ask themselves what their "skills and wills" are towards making the dream house a dream home.

I WANT TO BE HAPPY

When a boy and a girl decide to get married, they seldom think consciously about the advantageous division of labor which constitutes marriage. Most girls do not realize that romance is what they might be looking for in marriage. Most boys do not think very consciously about the sexual element of their desires, even though it might be quite strong. But everyone marries in the hope of obtaining happiness. The old love song which starts, "I want to be happy," is right.

Certainly this should not surprise us. St. Thomas Aquinas says that the urge to happiness is the motive which inspires every one of our actions. We can never want to be sad. We can never want to hurt ourselves. In our lifetime we want happiness most, and many young people choose marriage to give them happiness. Unfortunately, they too seldom know what kind of happiness marriage should give them. In fact, they don't even know what happiness is.

For many people happiness simply equals pleasure plus money. This is not surprising, since all our advertisements capitalize on this feeling. A cigarette advertisement reads, "Be happy, go Lucky." Another adds, "It is a psychologically established fact that pleasure improves your disposition." The logic here is that, since my disposition is improved, I must be happier. Just pick up any popular magazine and count the appeals to pleasure. Notice the kodachromed steaks, the appeals to "a new taste thrill," the subtle suggestion of sense pleasure— all definitely suggesting that happiness will flow from this or that pleasure.

Though pleasure can enhance our happiness, it cannot give happiness in itself. The crying child separated from his mother may be consoled with ice cream, but he cannot be made happy with it. The world is full of bored, weary people who have spent a lifetime in seeking happiness in pleasure.

The second half of the modern formula for happiness is money or the material things money can buy. Go through your newspaper again and see how many appeals are made to buy, own, borrow, rent, or use some material thing. When the automobile people cry, "Join the swing to swept wing" (or whatever the current slogan is), they imply in every rich, lush tone of the announcer that your happiness can be found in the most modern of cars. This applies to salesmen who sell everything from houses to television sets. Yet, how few of us are truly happy with all our material possessions.

The more gadgets we have, the more we seem to need, and somehow these gadgets tie us so close to themselves that we have no time for anything else. Recently I met a farmer who used to till one hundred acres, and was rather happy with his produce, despite the fact that he worked very hard. Then he thought he would take it a bit easier, and bought a lot of farm machinery. He discovered that though the work is easier with the machinery, he now must till two hundred acres and sell the produce in order to keep his machinery. He has discovered that material goods have merely put him on a treadmill trying to keep up with their demands.

Many a young father and husband has discovered the same thing. In order to get the material things which he thinks will make his life happy, he finds himself forced to work a job and a half, or two jobs. Sometimes he discovers that he must ask his wife to join him in working outside the home in order to have all these things. Frequently both of them are too tired to enjoy them, but the advertisements tell the couple that they are only happy if they have these material objects, and so they try to discover their blessedness in things.

In looking forward to their marriage, many young engaged people imagine themselves in a pleasant new ranch-style home with two or three pretty children dressed in lovely clothes and enjoying themselves with their pets on the lawn. The young wife-to-be sees her husband as a Prince Charming gradually growing into a distinguished gentleman. The young husband-to-be envisions his wife as a petite, attractive mother gradually growing into a dainty, vivacious matron. This is an attractive picture, but what will happen if it is not developed?

Suppose, as a matter of fact, that the pleasant home never materializes beyond a fourth floor apartment? Suppose the "pretty" children turn out to be ungainly, rope-haired youngsters? Suppose the only clothes you can give them are hand-me-downs from your relatives? Suppose the handsome gentleman remains a worn, harried provider? Suppose the petite woman, worn out by housework and child care, becomes haggard and wan? Will you, nevertheless, be happy?

What is *happiness*? Happiness is the mental state of the person who constantly possesses *good*. If, in your mind, this good means good things or good pleasures, you will never be happy because good things can never satisfy the human heart. Just think of last year's Christmas presents. Can you even remember what they were? Every good thing we have in a material way merely prepares the way for us to yearn for another good. Yearning is desire—not happiness. Again, pleasure can satisfy you only temporarily. Though you think you could enjoy mountains of ice cream, you soon find out that a small amount is more than sufficient. All pleasures are quickly exhausted.

What kind of happiness can marriage bring? Though it can bring material goods and pleasures (which *are* really good), it brings much more satisfaction when you seek the non-material goods inherent in it. Marriage is a *vocation*—the state of being called out of nothingness to love and serve. When you discover that you are fulfilling yourself in the love and service of wife or husband, of children and of God, the happiness that follows is indescribable. Happiness is discovered in the conscious possession of one's own full development as a man or woman, which means motherhood or fatherhood. It is the awareness of filling out one's potential for achievement. It is the knowledge of loving and being loved. It is a sense of achieving one's whole purpose of existence.

Even if the comfortable home, the beautiful children in lovely clothes, and the distinguished gentleman and his mature wife never materialize, even if poverty, unloveliness, and disaster will be your lot, you can still be happy. The challenge of maintaining your love in adversity; the sense of achievement in helping children to become adults, however lacking in intelligence or external attractiveness; the joy of knowing yourself to be fulfilling your love for God: these are sufficient to give endless happiness in your life. And this same happiness builds happiness for all eternity.

The song we quoted in the beginning of this article started, "I want to be happy." However, it continues, "but I can't be happy till I make you happy too." In marriage, happiness lies in giving joy and love to another: in giving joy and love to a husband or wife; in giving joy and love to children; in giving joy and love to God. Many people are afraid to give to others because they fear to lose from their own store. This can happen only with material goods. Happiness cannot be lost, because it is the only thing that can be multiplied in you by dividing it with others.

Chapter Two

QUALIFICATIONS

AIMING AT LOVE

Since marriage and family life bring with them such serious responsibilities, a great deal of preparation for this kind of life is imperative. A remote preparation demands that a person looking forward to marriage should develop the skills necessary to play the role of husband or wife, mother or father. It demands, moreover, an acceptance and even desire for the marital love-experience. It requires a clear realization that marriage is a God-made road to happiness in this life as well as a service of God which will deserve eternal reward. Lastly, it calls for a determination to live in marriage according to its founder's instructions. Thus prepared, a young man or woman is ready to fall into love.

Love is called the "grand passion." So it is. Love is indeed a wonderful passion. Yet the word "passion" points out a serious danger. Passion means something that we suffer or endure; something which happens to us whether we wish it or not. The passion of anger is something which happens to us. Very seldom is it a good thing to experience anger. Only occasionally when anger is guided by judgment, when we are *justly* angry, is the passion a good one. Again, passion often involves a *falling*. Falling is something over which we have little control. We usually dread and avoid physical falling, although in certain cases— parachuting from a crippled airplane, diving into a cool summer pool, performing as a trapeze artist—it can be a desirable or pleasant thing to choose. In the same way, emotional falling should also be a chosen thing and not merely something that happens. Before we fall into the passion of love, we need to take careful aim.

There is a difference between the action of love and the passion of love. The action of loving means that I wish well to someone else. I discover another self as dear and as close to me as I am to myself. My beloved's welfare is as important to me as my own. The Second Commandment —second to the one of loving God above all things—is to love my neighbor as I love myself. The act or habit of love is not always accompanied by the "grand passion." Love is not always thrilling. A mother who justly punishes a child; a wife who endures a harsh word from her husband; a husband who worries over his wife's health: are all actively in love, but there is no passion accompanying this love. Fortunate is the person whose active love is bolstered by the divine thrill, but eventually miserable is the person who falls into the passion of love without active love—and it can happen to you.

Since passion is something that happens to us, but love is something we want to *do*, it is most important that the head should guide the heart. Love is a tricky thing, and every young person should think carefully and long about the object of his love in order to discover whether it is truly lovable or not.

Equally, we should not accept the love of another unless we feel that we are a worthwhile object of love. If through self-awareness I find many faults in myself, it would only be fair to warn my beloved of them lest he enter into a lifelong union which might be disastrous.

Modern literature, both fictional and factual, is full of stories about unhappily married couples who did not take into account the kind of person they should have loved. The terms "incompatibility" and "emotional immaturity" pepper our literature on marriage and the family as explanations for disaster and divorce. It is only common sense to discover in one's self and in a potential mate all the qualities that should make a happy and holy marriage. After all, we have norms by which we choose our friends and acquaintances. Furthermore, we demand certain conditions for the places in which we work, and for the superiors for whom we are willing to do a job. We are even critical of members of our own family and prefer one to another. Why not, therefore, have norms and objective criticisms for the one with whom we might wish to spend an entire lifetime in the intimacy of marriage?

What are the qualities which you ought to have in order to marry? What are the qualities which you should demand of a possible future partner? If marriage is a way to get to heaven under God's direction, then both partners certainly should have very definite religious convictions and moral virtues. Secondly, since life together is a very intimate thing, there should be some sort of mutual compatibility and ability to adjust. If two people are all rough edges, they certainly will rub each other raw. Finally, since marriage is definitely for adults, a man and a woman intending to marry should have a reasonable mental, emotional, and physical maturity. A man and a woman who are still children in heart, in mind, or body can hardly make a good husband and wife, father and mother.

Though this all seems obvious, don't wait until you have fallen in love to check these qualifications; the passion of love can be blind. All through your growing years develop more and more clearly your ideas of what qualifications should be expected of a possible spouse. Then, when you meet a person who seems to be the "right one," you will be able to recognize whether he or she measures up to those ideals. If you have taken careful aim in this way, then—and only then—go ahead and love.

SOMETHING OF IMPORTANCE

Every boy or girl looking towards marriage pictures an ideal mate. That picture is like a pencil sketch, each stroke of which is a feature or trait to be sought in a possible life

partner. The first trait that should be in your picture is
religion. Since marriage is something invented by God,
and since it is a method of reaching Him, it is most important that your choice involve consideration of the religious practices of your future spouse. Does your intended
husband or wife share with you the ideal of a Christian
marriage? Does he or she truly desire to use the marital
state in order to reach heaven? Does your future spouse
desire to follow God's plan for happiness and holiness in
marriage? Does your intended believe that God has a
share in every action of your marriage?

To be more concrete, do you and your future husband
or wife believe that marriage is for life and is not to be
terminated at the whim or even serious wish of either
partner? Do you both accept the fact that artificial interference with the marriage act is a rejection of God's part
in procreation? Will children be begotten in and for God?
Will they be educated to take their places among the elect
of heaven? Be sure you can give favorable answers both
for yourself and for your partner. It would be most unwise to enter into a union which God Himself has established for definite purposes, unless you understood and
agreed on those purposes. How foolish would it be for you
to enter medical school if you did not want to heal the
sick! How ridiculous to become a social worker if you had
no concern for the welfare of other human beings!

The question of the religious awareness with which you
or your future spouse approach marriage applies very
seriously to the possibility of entering a mixed marriage,
but we shall treat this further on. Here, the same question
can be raised about Catholic marriages, since there are
many today who are Catholic in name only and who have
absorbed the secular approach to marriage from their environment. They believe that marriage is something invented merely for the convenience of any man and woman
who wish to live together. Their whole goal is to solve the
problem of loneliness in life, to reach some kind of divi-

sion of labor, to achieve sexual release, to discover romance, and to do nothing more. This attitude may even be relatively unconscious.

You should examine your own attitude to marriage and that of your future spouse, not only on the basis of your formal statements but also on your indirect beliefs as revealed from your words and actions regarding others. Suppose in a discussion about contraception the other person shows no concern that this is against the law of God. Suppose he or she speaks approvingly of divorce in a particular case. However much a person may protest that he accepts God's teaching, you cannot safely make a contract with someone who gives only lip service to the divine plan. If all the discussion between you is about furniture and receptions and the honeymoon and "getting ahead" and never a word is passed about God and children and supernatural life, beware! A lacy wedding gown is not so important as the "wedding garment" (divine grace) that Christ talks about.

You are baptized and confirmed, I presume, but how often do you go to Confession? How often do you receive Communion? Do you say your daily prayers—morning, night, before and after meals? Is Sunday Mass not only a duty but a joyful privilege for you? If you are only an "Easter duty" Catholic you may be ready for a mere human mating, but you are not ready for Christian wedlock.

It frequently happens that one partner in an engagement changes his way of life during courtship, after years of ignoring God and His faith. A young man may suddenly "get religion" when he falls in love. Obviously this could be equally true about the young woman. But how deep is the conversion? Is it just an external observance to please and win a beloved? Such a "conversion" should be carefully examined and tested both by the "convert" and the fervent Catholic he or she wishes to marry. It certainly would not be fair for someone to enter into a contract of marriage on the basis of mere external change.

It would be utterly foolhardy for a convinced, active Catholic to marry such a convert without proof that the change was deep and permanent.

Though lack of religious conviction is of concern chiefly because of the vocational meaning of Christian marriage, it should be almost as important on the basis of temporal happiness. Modern marriage experts talk about mutual compatibility and adjustment. This usually means mutual interest in things of importance. It is quite impossible to make even a temporally happy marriage between two people who are not mutually interested in what is of fundamental importance in their lives. A man who looks down on his wife as a mere pietistic church-goer, or a religious woman married to a near-atheist cannot carry on a really deep conversation. There is no basic point of view held in common. A man who is intensely concerned with the Mystical Body of Christ and his necessary activity in it will find it extremely difficult to adjust to a woman who is utterly indifferent to religious practice. Even the secular experts are discovering that however much they themselves do not accept religion as part of marriage, religious difference can be a very serious source of disharmony in family life.

From the point of view of both eternal and temporal happiness then, religion is an important foundation for a successful marriage. Make sure that the picture you carry in your heart of your ideal mate has strong religious coloring. Furthermore, be just as anxious when you look into the mirror of your own conscience to discover the same coloring there.

DON'T GET MIXED UP

Every citizen of the United States, whether Catholic, Protestant, or Jew, knows that the Catholic Church is opposed to marriage between people of different faiths.

Few, however, realize the reasons behind this objection. Non-Catholics, and even some Catholics, think that the Church cares only about losing members. They imply that she is concerned with membership statistics only in order to be able to boast about the number of Catholics in the world. True, the Church is worried about leakage, but not simply because she wants to boast of the number of her communicants, or to get bigger collections on Sunday morning. She wants every man, woman, and child to reach heaven, and she wants each to walk the same road to that destination.

More souls are lost to Catholicism and to God through mixed marriages than from any other source. Reliable studies indicate that approximately twenty-five per cent of all valid mixed marriages are lost completely to God, and another twenty per cent attend church services only from time to time. Somewhere from five to twenty per cent of the children of mixed marriages are not even baptized, and from thirty to forty per cent receive no formal instruction in their faith! These frightening statistics are not drawn solely from Catholic sources. Even a Methodist, Dr. Leiffer, says, "The most common pattern in marriages between people of different religious backgrounds is the development of indifference towards the Church. Not only is religion omitted from conversation, it does not enter significantly into the thinking of the parents. Usually this is reflected in lack of religious training for the children."

Of course, many who read this article will say, "I know many mixed marriages which have worked." Even if I were to grant that this were true (and fortunately often is true), is this how you would like to describe what you now think is triumphant love? Suppose I ask you, "How do you like your car?" If you answer with a shrug, "It works," would this be high praise? If I ask you, "How do you like your job?" and you answer, "It's work," would this show any enthusiasm for your way of earning a living? In the same way, talking about mixed marriages "which work" is hardly to praise them. The real question is not "Can a mixed marriage work?" but "Can a mixed marriage be fully and completely happy, even from the temporal point of view?"

For a Catholic, marriage is a miniature union—a reliving in the twentieth century—of Christ and His Church. How could this possibly be realized when one partner might not even recognize Christ and His Church? Love by its very nature seeks union. If one partner in a marriage is not a member of Christ's Body, the Church, there will always be part of the Catholic partner which cannot be united to the non-Catholic. Pope Pius XI says, "There will be wanting [in a mixed marriage] that close union of spirit which, as it is the sign and mark of the Church of Christ, so also should it be the sign of Christian wedlock, its glory and adornment."

St. Paul says, "Wives, be subject to your husbands as to the Lord," and in another verse, "Husbands, love your wives as Christ also loved the Church." In true Catholic thinking, could Christ be truly and completely united with one who will not accept all or even part of His teaching? If He cannot, neither can a Catholic husband or wife be truly and completely united with their non-Catholic spouse.

Just recently, a young mother came up to me and said, "Father, I have not met you personally, but you have been haunting me for the past five years!" I was amazed and asked what she meant. She answered, "I heard you give a talk five years ago in another city. The question was asked whether mixed marriages could be truly and completely happy. You answered, 'Though a mixed marriage can be reasonably successful, I do not believe that it can be truly and perfectly happy because the whole norm of perfect unity, the unity of Christ and His Church, cannot be achieved in it.'"

"At that time, Father," she continued, "I was ready to get up and object vigorously, because I was in a mixed marriage then and considered myself very happy. But since that time your words have been ringing through my mind again and again. Finally, I took instructions and became a Catholic just a year ago." I said to her, "My dear, I have only one question for you. *Was I right?*" This lovely lady simply looked into my eyes with a depth of meaning that I cannot put on paper and said, "Yes."

Therefore, don't get mixed up! As a Catholic, envision yourself married only to a Catholic. A Catholic marriage will safeguard and develop your own faith; it will protect your partner's faith. It will insure Baptism and Christian education for each of your children. Finally, a Catholic marriage will open your love to a triumphant unity—full, complete, happy, and holy.

PRINCIPLES AND PRACTICES

There is an old saying that "a leopard can never change his spots." It refers to the well-known fact that people who have constantly spent their lives in sin do not easily become saints. Another saying expresses the same thing, "you cannot make a silk purse from a sow's ear." Fortunately these sayings are only half true. Experience shows that people who live a life of sin often never leave it, but nevertheless, with the help of penance and God's grace, conversion is possible for anyone. Christ has redeemed all mankind, and every man can change his life, turn over a new leaf, and become not only a good person, but even a saint. From the earliest times of the Church, great sinners have become great saints.

However, when it comes to marrying such a person, it is most important to make sure that the conversion has already taken place. Generally speaking, it is not wise to marry a former drunkard or one given over to impurity or dishonesty. If marriage is a way of getting to heaven, then each person ought to choose a partner who will help and not hinder him on the road. Marriage to one who has been addicted to all sorts of evil habits is hardly a worth-while risk. Someone has said that though it may not be *impossible* for one partner in a marriage to be saved without the other one, it is extremely *difficult*. Good moral character in your spouse, therefore, is a definite requirement before you say "I do."

Many married people have disregarded this requirement, to their sorrow. People who have thrown themselves away on a beloved without taking careful aim discover that falling in love is no sign that the object of the love is worth marrying. Many a drunkard, small-time gambler, petty thief, lascivious playboy has reformed in order to marry someone with whom he has fallen in love—only to return to his old ways of living after the newness of romantic love has faded. Many a bitter, angry, selfish, and spoiled young woman has changed her ways to please her "man," only to revert to type after the honeymoon was over.

How can you discover the moral qualities of a future partner? There is very little problem if the other person has lived a moral life for years. Though it is possible to fall into serious sins, and even the habit of sin, in later years, usually we will continue to live the kind of life that we have in the past. It is usually safer, therefore, to marry someone who has always lived an actively Christian life.

But suppose one falls in love with a person who has not been very good up to this time, but who now professes that he has been converted and will change his ways. How can you tell if this conversion is real, deep, and permanent? Try to discover whether the convert has changed merely to win your affections. It is easy to change *practices* to meet the demands of a beloved when the fundamental *principles* of one's life have not changed at all. One could easily give up drinking in order to win a bet or to please a mother or father, and still have in one's heart the principle that drinking, or even drunkenness, is desirable. The practice of sobriety to achieve a temporary goal proves nothing. Just as soon as the goal is reached, the original principle will go into effect.

In the same way, as soon as marriage is achieved, someone who has changed his way of life to win a partner may well revert to his previous type of life. Therefore, try to discover whether the *principle* of your beloved's life has been changed, not just a temporary practice. This is something that must be proved in action, not by words alone. Watch carefully to discover whether this principle is exemplified at all times, not merely when you are there to observe it. See whether your prospective convert from evil living talks just as clearly about right and wrong in relation to others as he does in relation to himself. A girl who believes that divorce might be right for a friend, may well decide, at some future date, that divorce could be right for her, even though now she may protest that she cannot conceive of such a situation. A man who condones unjust business practices by his friends may well excuse himself for the same practices later, even though now he may assert that such a consideration would never enter his mind.

Though it is possible "for a leopard to change his spots," don't take it for granted when you decide to pledge your life to another for all time!

SOUNDNESS OF BODY

In your picture of the ideal mate, there should certainly be an element of normally robust health. Marriage and family life can take a great toll of one's physical resources. Bearing a child, though it is a normal physiological fact and by no means a sickness, is nevertheless not something to be undertaken lightly. Good physical condition is necessary. To support a family, to keep a home in good order, to bear the strain and worry of sleepless nights with sick children, to get up at two in the morning for a feeding or to give a child a "drink of water," is not easy for even the most robust. It becomes almost impossible for those who are in poor health. Common sense, then, demands that you choose as your partner in marriage someone reasonably healthy and that you give yourself to that partner with the health necessary for the performance of your functions as husband or wife, father or mother.

Does this mean that only athletes should marry? Certainly not. Those who have great physical strength or athletic ability are not necessarily as healthy as they seem. But I do mean that a young man should ask himself whether he is equal to the task of supporting a family; a young woman should ask herself whether she can bear children without danger to her life and whether she can take on the burdens of daily child-care.

Those planning to get married should make their general physical condition a topic of discussion before marriage. Should a couple discover that they are not as physically fit as they should be, they may still marry, but they should have their eyes wide open to the sacrifices that their disabilities might entail. If a tubercular man contracts marriage, his wife should understand that he might not be able to work hard enough to support her and the children in the style she might desire. He would have to guard his energies carefully and such things as overtime work might be impossible. If a woman enters marriage with a serious heart ailment, both she and her husband should understand the possible necessity of long periods of absolute continence which her condition might demand. Her heart trouble might require a great deal of housework from her husband, who could not justly claim that this was only "woman's work."

In order to discover the state of your health before marriage, take this advice. Have a physician give you a complete head-to-toe examination. Don't be content merely to have your pulse counted, your heartbeat listened to, and your blood pressure checked. This is not a good physical examination! A good examination should include a chest x-ray, a blood count, and many other routine procedures. To show why this is important let me tell you of a personal experience.

In preparing a group of couples for marriage I became quite friendly with one young couple and, after the series of lectures was over, took it for granted they would soon marry. When I met them eighteen months later and asked them how their marriage was going, they told me, to my surprise, that they were not yet married. I asked why, and the young woman replied: "Father, as a result of your suggestions on physical preparedness for marriage, we both went for a complete physical examination. Bob discovered he had a hidden diabetic condition which was very serious. It was far along, and if we had married according to plan, he might have gone into a coma and perhaps even died on our honeymoon. It has taken all these months to control the diabetic condition with insulin, and we are still debating the advisability of marriage, even though we still love each other very much. At least we are going to be able to face the situation when we do march down the aisle."

Of course, no one has any guarantee that since he is healthy now he will be healthy for the rest of his life. All sorts of risks must be taken in marriage, and the risk of future illness is one which love should be ready to face. But it is no more than reasonable foresight to check one's physical condition and that of one's partner before marriage.

Generally speaking, any couple who wants to get married has the right to do so, but, still, only those with reasonable health should marry. If a person with a serious physical handicap wishes to marry despite the contrary indications, his proposed partner should know the facts.

Both should show clear willingness to accept the sacrifices which might be involved for them in living with this physical condition.

MARRIAGE IS FOR ADULTS

Are you mature enough for marriage? What makes you sure that you are? Most engaged couples take their maturity for granted. After all, you are twenty-one or more years of age. You have completed your schooling, are working at what looks like a steady job, are sound in body and feel yourself in the pink of condition. But is this enough maturity for marriage?

No matter how old we are, how rich our experiences, how much we have lived, we are all somewhat immature because maturity is a relative term. As we work through the problems of a lifetime from birth to death, each of our experiences should help us to become more and more adult. Since it is possible to grow more and more mature with every year of life, only death should stop our maturing process. However, many people stop their maturing at a certain age-level. Not only do they stop growing physically at a certain age, but some refuse to learn any more from experience. Such people are already dead even though they may be many years from burial!

To your parents, who have lived and learned together for many years, you engaged couples seem very immature. They are right. You have many more years of maturing to live. It has taken you some twenty or more years to face up to the simple responsibility of "popping the question." It will take you more years of growing to meet the responsibilities of child care, mutual faults, illnesses, and growing old together. At your present point, you need not be mature enough to die, but you should have enough maturity to begin a new kind of maturing which is family life.

Marriage experts agree that the greatest enemy of success and happiness in marriage is not poverty, bodily weakness, sexual incompatibility, parental interference, but *emotional immaturity*. They insist that they find such undeveloped personalities not only among those who marry young but also among those who marry after years of worldly experience and even in couples who are celebrating their silver wedding anniversary! Unfortunately, though some experts can describe cases of emotional immaturity, few if any of them can define what it is.

Emotional immaturity can be described in one word—childishness. Notice that I say "childishness"—not "childlikeness." Would to God that more spouses were childlike. A childlike personality is one who has simple, clear, naive vision, who speaks candidly and is not devious or full of duplicity, who is not confused about goals in life but pursues the important ones simply. On the other hand many adults, indeed all of us at one time or another, exhibit childish traits. We are an easy prey to jealousy, temper tantrums, petty rivalries, grasping selfishness. If we are honest with ourselves we will take a lifetime to discover and root out all the childish traits to which human nature is heir. We camouflage our emotional immaturity with all sorts of "reasonable" excuses.

Since all of us are more or less emotionally immature, how can you engaged couples discover whether you are mature enough for marriage? There are a number of tests you can give yourself. Are you big enough to recognize childishness when you find it in yourself and to be ashamed enough of it to correct yourself? Are you still subject to temper tantrums that can be triggered by the most innocent remark? Do you indulge in the more adult equivalent of the spoiled brat's tongue-wagging? Are you so jealous that your future spouse must account for every moment away from you? Are you so insecure in love that no amount of protestations will satisfy you? Then you are still emotionally immature. We are not surprised when a child throws a temper tantrum and kicks his heels on the floor when his wishes are crossed, yet it is shocking to discover many mothers of children who manifest their "tantrums" by unreasonable tears, petty nagging, or harping upon some fancied slight. It is pretty sad to see a muscular, terrible-tempered Mr. Bang explode into shouting and cursing. It is sadly ridiculous to observe both of them pointedly ignoring each other when they give each other the endless "silent treatment." It is utterly incongruous to see a fully developed man and woman acting out a camouflaged version of the childish, "I don't want to play in your yard."

Are you free of excessive dependence on your parents? Do you always blame someone else for your failures? When a child of three is bored on a rainy afternoon, we expect him to ask, "What shall I do now, Mommy?" When he falls and hurts himself, we take it for granted that Mother should kiss his tears away; when he fails to accomplish a task or is caught in some childish fault, we are not upset when he complains, "Jimmy wouldn't let me," or "I couldn't help it." However, it is utterly shocking to see these equivalents in someone entering marriage. There are many young men and women who cannot come to a decision without having their decision made for them by their parents. Others never feel sure that they should proceed until their parents have fully approved. Still more childish are those grown-ups who make rash decisions and then run off and expect parents, friends, or spouses to cover for their foolishness or to console them when they have failed. Most exasperating are the young people who blame everyone but themselves for their failures: "The boss wouldn't back me up." "My wife nagged me to quit." "Somebody knifed me." Cry-babies are not old enough for marriage.

What kind of value-system do you have? Are childish and adolescent pleasures your chief goal in life? Children and adolescents like pleasure. We are not surprised when children and adolescents look for their happiness in a picnic, a roller-coaster ride, an afternoon in the fun house, a pretty toy, a collection of cheap records, or a thrilling movie. But we should be surprised at adults who still find all their joys in a few pleasant childish values. Some young couples will blow a week's budget for an evening out in an expensive restaurant followed by orchestra seats at a musical. Others will go into debt for a color TV set and watch it from a few rickety chairs. One young couple started their marriage with a three thousand dollar debt on a red and white convertible which they watched ticking away like a taxi-meter in depreciation, while they could scarcely find enough money for gasoline to go back and forth to work! One young marriage foundered and broke apart because the husband insisted on a thousand dollars' worth of photographic equipment while his medical fees for the first baby were left unpaid.

Do not protest that your values are mature until you have actually checked them. Supermarkets admittedly keep solvent by carefully displaying overpriced luxury items before the childish eyes of a million impulse buyers.

Are you mature enough for marriage? You are if, *first*, you can talk out your frustrations calmly and if you can learn to see another person's point of view. *Second*, you are mature if, after seeking advice, you can make up your own mind and accept success with joy, and failure without crying over spilt milk. *Third*, you are mature enough for marriage if you can postpone or do without a present pleasure while pursuing worthwhile long-range goals.

Chapter Three

DIFFERENCES

WHAT THE DIFFERENCE IS

According to the dictionary, sex is the quality of being male or female. Such a definition applies to plants, animals, and human beings. It merely describes the physical differences which enable two different principles to contribute to the begetting of progeny, whether this progeny be seeds, pups, or infants. For human beings this definition is extremely inadequate. For human beings sex should mean the quality of being *masculine* or *feminine*.

A man is a man and a woman is a woman in every fiber of the being of each. Every cell in a man's body is marked masculine. Every cell in a woman's body is marked feminine. However, not only are their bodies different, but their emotions, their manner of thinking, their manner of practicing virtue, their method of loving, even their religious experiences are quite different.

A man's body is marked not only by the physical apparatus for begetting offspring, but also by his strength and build. A man is built for strong, muscular exertion. It doesn't take much proving to show that the average man is physically stronger than the average woman. A woman's body, on the other hand, is marked not only by the function of child-bearing, but by her muscular and physical build. A woman is built for endurance, not for speed or strength. Her endurance shows in the endless tiny tasks which she is expected to do in daily life. Most men would be physically exhausted by an ordinary day in a houseful of children. Because of such a simple difference as skeleton articulation, a woman can touch her toes long after middle age, whereas a man can no longer do this when he has lost the suppleness of youth.

Men and women are different in their emotional structures, too. A woman tends to express only the "softer" emotions. She can pity, cry, be sad, express love and affection much more easily than can a man. On the other hand, a man expresses the "harder" emotions. He can get angry, become aggressive, express stubbornness. Even when they express the same emotions, they usually do so differently. A man tends to get angry with his fists. He wants to slam doors and give strong physical expression to his anger. A woman gets angry much more slowly and much more quietly. We describe her anger as "a slow burn." A man's anger mounts quickly and fades rapidly. A woman's anger rises slowly, comes to a boil, and takes a long time to cool off.

Popular cartoon opinion not withstanding, women think as well as men—but they think differently. A man thinks in logical progression from abstract principles. He talks about justice, charity, peace, world order. He defines and distinguishes endlessly. On her side a woman thinks in concrete and personal terms. Her thoughts and language are full of proper names like John, Mary, Irene, and so on. A man tends to listen to the ideas expressed in a conversation. A woman is inclined to listen to the person who expresses the thoughts.

And so it goes with the rest of the personality of man and woman. Certain virtues come easier to a woman, others easier to a man. Certain religious experiences are more natural to a woman, others more natural to a man. Because of the ease and enthusiasm with which a woman takes up virtuous and religious living, many men feel that their wives are pietistic. Because of the hesitancy with which a man faces religion and virtuous living, many women are afraid that their husbands are almost irreligious. Neither fear is justified. It is simply a matter of a man's growing in virtue in masculine fashion and a woman's growing in virtue in feminine fashion—and both of them should accept the different growths of each other.

The frequency with which men and women fall in love and marry would seem to indicate that people know the differences between the sexes and want to experience these differences. Certainly, they should want to complement each other's lacks, and yet they seem disappointed when they discover their differences in marriage. After an argument with his wife, a man will stamp out saying to himself, "I'll never understand women." In concluding the same argument a woman will cry out in frustration, "Men!" The husband and wife seem to be surprised and disappointed that they have two different approaches to a discussion. It would almost seem that a man would prefer another man as his partner in marriage and a woman would prefer another woman!

Still, there is no doubt that a young man and young woman very much want the differences between them in order to fill out their respective needs. The mystery of man and the mystery of woman is an attractive thing to explore for a lifetime together. Yet, since they do not know fully what they wish, they frequently stop working at mutual understanding in marriage and drift into their aloneness again.

By all means go into marriage determined to enjoy your masculine and feminine differences for a lifetime. This attitude should be a tremendous benefit to the young bride and groom—one which brings intense joy and pleasure through the constant discovery of new facets in their masculinity and femininity. Be more feminine and more masculine and love the difference! Encourage the differences. Only a man who continues to become more manly and a woman who continues to become more womanly can continue together to be a better husband and wife, father and mother.

DREAMS AND THE MAN

The natural gift of the masculine person is devotion to a cause or an ideal. A man envisions a plan which he wishes to put into effect during his lifetime. The tremendous basic urge in his character is to make a dent in the community, to realize a competence, to make the world better for his having existed.

Because he has this devotion to an ideal, and longs to achieve it, he is naturally quite aggressive. He is also domineering; he will aways insist that he has the right answer. Since he is aggressive and domineering, the masculine temperament will give him the courage, over the long distance, to work towards his goal. He may well have a long-range plan of several years, and his courage in patiently plodding through it is one of his key characteristics. A man is also interested in things. Since he must take his place in the world of creation by changing that world, he becomes interested in the machinery, the equipment, the inventions which will enable him to change things.

Lastly, a man is an unconfessed dreamer. He has stupendous aspirations for the future. He plans a wonderful home for his wife and his children. He anticipates climbing the ladder of success to become a general manager, an office-holder in political life, a popular speaker, a labor organizer, an eminent lawyer, a prominent doctor, etc.

Why does a man possess these characteristics? Because his function as a masculine person is to be a provider and a planner. He must provide for the needs of the world. Since he seems to have been called into the world to make it a better place in which to live, his constant craving is to render valuable service to his family and to the community. Yet, when a man sees the reality of his life, he feels a profound sense of frustration and discouragement. After twenty-five years of promising his wife financial security and a beautiful mortgage-free home in the suburbs, he discovers that he is still kissing her good-evening in the fourth floor walk-up for which they are paying sky-high rent. After years of dedication to the labor movement, a union member will find that he is merely recognized as "a good Joe" and is never given any opportunity to exercise the leadership for which he yearns. After hard work to earn public recognition as a lawyer or a political worker, many a man finds himself still at the foot of the ladder, and no one ever seems to notice his worth. When a man comes home at night with slumped shoulders and dragging steps, the cause is not so much that he is weary and exhausted physically, as it is that he has apparently failed another day.

For all these reasons a wife must be a very wise woman in order to give her husband happiness. She must learn to exhilarate him, magnify his ability, encourage him each evening so that he can go out to meet the challenge of another day and conquer the world. No man is ever truly a failure until his wife deems him so. Once she has taken for granted that he will never get anywhere, once she has stopped encouraging him, his day of achievement has faded beyond the horizon.

In order to give her husband a sense of competence and leadership a wise woman must seek his judgment, even if she has her own mind made up. A clever wife will also refuse to take over the management of her home. She will force her husband into the leadership, not by demanding, in so many words, that he take the lead, but by creating a vacuum in the area of decisions until he assumes the responsibility.

Above all, young bride, once you are married never laugh at his dreams! If he is no longer telling you about his hopes and plans for the following day; if he no longer relishes your concern for his new efforts, it is because you have belittled him. By word or example you have said with disgust in your voice, "Yes, I've heard all those dreams before. When are you going to stir yourself and produce?" A wife's lack of confidence breeds failure in her husband.

Isn't it interesting how well we know methods of hurting and how little we use the same knowledge to express love? A woman quickly learns how to needle her husband. Among a group of people she will belittle him and his efforts. She will imply that he is an old miser, a skinflint, a bad lover, an ineffectual provider. If you watch the others as you talk and then cast an eye in the direction of her husband, you will notice his uneasiness and the onset of anger. Above all, a man hates to appear a failure before others.

Women should remember that a man has an infinite capacity for taking praise. He doesn't desire adulation and untruths, but he yearns to have you find in him some perfection, some accomplishment for which you can laud him and in which he can take pleasure and feel successful. A man will recognize a charming woman as "one who notices me."

If a husband does not feel this sense of competence, of belonging in his own home, he will seek it outside his home. There is a place on every street corner where he can secure a sense of success and belonging. Behind a long mahogany counter there stands a man in a white apron who for a few cents (the price of a beer) will tell him that he is wonderful and his wife doesn't really understand him. If such a husband has enough money in his pockets to "set them up for the boys," the entire male fraternity present will listen to his stories. Why shouldn't he go out to the corner bar with someone to listen to him, if no one at home pays any attention to him?

If he doesn't go to the bar to get his sense of success, he will inevitably wend his way to his mother. All his life he has found that she believes in him, thinks he is wonderful, and extols his achievements.

A last resort is business. Many men who find no encouragement at home become so engrossed in their bank account, the position that they take among their fellows in business, the success of their company, that they practically marry the business and leave their wife and children alone.

The key to an understanding of the masculinity of a man is an understanding of his profound need for creative ideals. If you want to know why he is happy, ask yourself how he has succeeded. If you want to know why he is sad, ask yourself, "How have I, or how has his environment, offended his sense of being a success?" Men fear failure above all else.

PERSON TO PERSON

Where a man's natural devotion is to a cause or a plan, a woman is naturally *devoted to her beloved*. Whereas a man can become enthusiastic over a theory or an idea, a woman's attachment is usually only to persons, toward whom she easily develops deep loyalties. A ready sympathy, a great deal of understanding, and deep tenderness for her beloved emanate from such loyalty. Because a woman is so lost in personality, she is also gifted in the details which surround persons.

I once met a couple who had just left their boy at college. On their arrival there, the father had been invited to go into the dormitory to see his son's room. Of course, the mother was quite chagrined to discover that women were not allowed in the building. When her husband returned, she questioned him minutely about each detail in her son's room and was exasperated to find that he had observed only the usual desk, two chairs, a window, and a bed. I thought I knew why she was irritated, and when I asked her the reason, her reply went something like this: "When I am away from someone that I love, I want to be able to see him in precisely the situation where he is. I want to see him sprawled in his arm-chair. I want to observe the book in his hands. I want to share the view he sees from his window. I want to know in concrete terms how comfortable his bed is. Only when I share these details of his life do I feel personally near him. My husband is content to know that our son is popular, successful, and proficient academically. I want to know who his friends are, what the triumphs and failures of his life are, etc."

Why does a woman have this natural endowment of devotion to her beloved? Because, Pope Pius XII teaches, "She is called by nature to be a mother, either in fact or in spirit." It is this natural "motherhood" that makes a woman such a good teacher, nurse, or social worker. It also explains her deftness in dealing with juveniles in the courtroom. The male judge tends to make the punishment fit the crime, and the defense of law and justice is paramount in his mind. On the other hand, the feminine judge is more inclined to make the punishment fit the criminal, and the needs of the young delinquent will be paramount in her judgment.

In the field of pedagogy a man tends to teach a subject. He loses himself in mathematics, history, or biology; he adapts his words to the thought content of these subjects. Because a woman becomes engrossed in personalities, she usually teaches a person and adapts each of her words to the particular needs of the individual student.

A woman centers her life around love, and she wants to be loved in return. Since she has such a profound need of love, she frequently experiences a gnawing fear that she is not loved or that she might not even be lovable. This apprehension causes a pervasive feeling of being left alone. Therefore, young husbands, your first duty to your wife is to take away her sense of loneliness. Notice your wife! A woman can take almost anything from a man except being taken for granted. If she asks you, "Dear, do you still love me?" she is showing you her need to be loved. When you hear this question, you can be certain that you have not told her of your love and affection for a long, long time.

Your usual answer to this question is not satisfactory: "Of course I love you. Why do you think I married you?"

A wife needs attention in a complimentary way from her husband, and she needs it in great detail. Compliment her on her efficient housekeeping and on her attractiveness. Compliment her on a fine meal, but make sure you mention *details*. If she has prepared the entire meal, from soup to dessert, completely around your own particular likes and you should happen to comment only on the pie, she will wonder whether you noticed the Hollandaise sauce, the rare cut of beef, the choice brand of coffee, and all the other details that equally show she loves you.

It is interesting to notice how many men understand the nature of women when they want to tease or even hurt their wives. They easily concentrate on details then, but ignore these same details when they should be expressing love. A man who wishes to tease his wife will say, "Dear, aren't you getting a bit fat?" He knows that the detail of "fat" will irritate his wife very much. Why is she irritated? Does she feel that her extra weight is slowing her down? No, she can still manage a flight of stairs. She is not worrying about the extra poundage in itself. But she is concerned about whether her husband still loves her with that extra weight! A wife wants to be lovable above all, and what does her teasing husband tell her? He subtly suggests that she is a little less lovable in proportion to her additional pounds.

When a man no longer gives his wife a sense of being loved, what happens in marriage? To mitigate her loneliness a wife turns first to her children. She knows that she is indispensable to them and realizes also that they will respond to all the affection that she lavishes upon them. Yet the affection of the children will never satisfy her, since they are only children and cannot respond to her adult needs. If her need for love does not "marry her to the children," she will perhaps find an emotional outlet by losing herself in soap-opera programs. Or she may seek love and affection from her own parents and be constantly visiting them in order to alleviate the dire sense of emptiness she feels as the result of the real or imagined loss of her husband's love.

Husbands, remember that a woman is concerned with all the details which surround her beloved, and that she looks for a great deal of detail in your concern for her. Use this understanding to express your love for her. Make sure you do not use it to tease or hurt her love.

A LANGUAGE DIFFICULTY

A man and woman who marry from a similar cultural background expect to speak the same language to each other. In the United States, they expect that their American brand of English will be quite satisfactory for verbal communication. However, it doesn't take long in marriage for husband and wife to suspect that, though the words each uses can be found in the English dictionary, the actual meanings of their sentences are quite different. In many ways men and women speak different languages. Someone has said this very pungently, "To understand a man, listen to exactly what he says; to understand a woman, don't listen to what she says but to what she *means*!"

Let's listen in on a conversation of young newly-weds who have not discovered this important foreign language which each spouse speaks. Husband and wife are relaxing together for a few moments before they go out for the evening. She quietly asks, "Dear, are you wearing that grey suit tonight?" What she is subtly suggesting is the following, "I hope you don't intend to embarrass me in front of my friends by wearing that ragged, unpressed business suit you have on now, do you?" He, being totally unversed in feminine linguistics, casually returns, "Yes, I am." When these three words are drained of every possible meaning and translated into what he really wanted to say, it is simply that, yes, he is wearing the grey suit. However, he does not have another man to make the translation, so his feminine interpreter has read the following meaning into those three simple words: "Yes, I intend to wear this suit despite the fact that I recognize it needs a pressing, and I don't care a bit about your friends."

The wife does not continue the conversation with a simple request. She doesn't say, "As a special favor to me so that I can hold my head up among my friends, would you mind changing into your tan slacks and sport coat?" Instead, she says, "You always looked so attractive in that tan sports combination!" When this has been translated into what she is really saying, it comes out, "Would you please not be so exasperating and change into your best clothes right now before I blow my stack?"

Still thinking that she is only making conversation, he now completes the confusion of language and utterly disconcerts his loving spouse by the calm observation, "I look just as good in the grey." Since this in interpreted to mean that he doesn't care what she thinks about his attire, he should not be terribly surprised if she bursts into tears and complains that he doesn't love her any more, and here they are married only these three weeks!

It should not surprise us to discover this difference in language between the sexes. Jesus and Mary in the New Testament manifested this same characteristic masculine and feminine approach in their use of words. In the New Testament at the wedding feast of Cana, Mary being the warm, tender mother she was, noticed that the young couple was embarrassed at the short supply of wine. She turned to Jesus and said, "They have no wine." It takes little thought to realize that she meant much more than she said. She was not coldly observing a fact; she was saying, in effect, "I notice the terrible embarrassment of this young couple since they are running out of wine, and it would please me a great deal if you would use your divine powers to make them happy."

Jesus replied in characteristically masculine fashion, "Woman, what is it to Me and to Thee. My hour [for miracles] has not yet come." Probably most women who read these lines suspect that our Lord was giving to His mother a curt refusal, whereas, as a matter of fact, He was simply stating that the time for His public ministry—and hence the time for miracles—was only on the point of beginning and it had not, as yet, been officially opened.

Did Mary then plead or ask directly for her miracle? No. She turned to the stewards and said to them, "Whatever He tells you to do, do." Here again we find the characteristic indirectness of a woman. Her confident loving request was manifested in the manner in which she put her divine son "on the spot."

All this shows that our Lord and our Lady were fully masculine and feminine and lived out these characteristics to the full.

How strange it is that a young man and young woman entering marriage and strongly attracted by each other's manly and womanly differences so seldom discover how to communicate through language. The young husband shows disappointment that his wife does not speak the language of the male fraternity. He wanted a bride and is surprised to find that she thinks like a woman! Many a young wife finds herself complaining that her husband is "just like a man." What else did she want in marriage except a man?

Instead of being a source of frustration, differences between the sexes in their use of words should provide a delightful challenge in mutual understanding. How boring if both used the same plodding and unimaginative masculine words! How utterly exasperating if both used the mysterious hidden-meaning approach!

Just as the learning of Italian, French, or Spanish can open up to us a whole new culture, with all its differences, so an awareness of the languages which men and women use, foreign each to the other, can be a delightful excursion into the endless quest for knowledge regarding the differences between men and women. It should be an interesting challenge to learn each other's language for a lifetime of communication.

ARE THE DIFFERENCES GOOD OR BAD?

Look through any modern book on marriage and you'll find a large portion of it directed toward a description of "adjustment." Most of the space in such chapters is concerned with developing mutual tastes and a broad background of agreements. There have even been attempts to match boys and girls for marriage with IBM machines which record levels of intelligence and background. This is really a new development in thought. We used to believe that men and women were different and that marriage was a union of differences. We used to believe that the old rhyme about Mr. and Mrs. Jack Spratt and their different tastes in meat was an indication that mates should be complementary rather than that they should be similar. The modern scheme of things revolves around the idea that the unity is one which is founded upon the elimination of differences rather than the unity of dissimilar personalities brought to a common fruitfulness by achieving the full development of their differences and in sharing different functions as man and wife, father and mother.

This makes marriage adjustment a matter of discovering a common denominator into which the differences of man and woman may be divided. This means that, if I like jazz and you like classical music, we can only make a marriage adjustment if both forget our tastes and learn to become middle-brows together. If I like my meat and potatoes well seasoned and you like yours without seasoning, our only adjustment can be if I will lose some of my taste for spices and you will achieve some taste for them.

Happiness does not depend upon sharing the same books or smoking the same brand of cigarettes! All that needs to be common to a man and wife is a common faith, common sense, a common bed and board, and common children. Beyond these, the only other common interests that might help cement the marriage bond would be those which are normally common to a man and woman. Since a man and a woman are different, have different functions, and different natural interests, there will not be too many of these common interests.

Sometimes a young couple is told to play the same games together. If the basis of marriage harmony is playing the same games, you may be sure that it will be a losing game, one in which it will become more and more the custom for one "child" to pick up the marbles and look for another playmate. To say that marriage is a companionship or a matter of mutual adjustment is the same kind of a lie as saying that Christ was a good man. In each case we are rejecting the reality involved by considering seriously only one aspect of it.

What is adjustment? To understand it fully, we need to know that it comes from two Latin words, "ad" and "juste", which means "justice towards." Adjustment therefore means a full willingness by a couple to recognize the human, personal values of each other and to meet each other's needs, even, if necessary, with a sense of cold justice. Adjustment does not mean that a man will be interested in what his wife will be interested in, but it does mean that he will be interested in her interest! This is not merely a play on words. A woman is naturally interested in babies. Each and every detail in their growth will call for loving awareness in her. A man, too, will be interested in his children's growth, but he cannot be expected to show the same thrill for each gurgle and burp that his wife does. It is, however, imperative for him to encourage and show pride in his wife's development as a mother. On her side, a woman cannot be expected to be as interested in the labor movement as her worker husband. Working conditions, "right to work" laws, and encyclicals on labor and capital will hardly be her cup of tea. The important thing is not that she desire a joint position as steward in her husband's union, but that she show her pride and interest in his growth and development as a labor leader.

Courtship is the time to discover all the differences in the natures of man and woman and all the unique individual differences that any two people have. Any attempt for a man and a woman to discover their *equality* is doomed to disappointment. You cannot say that a woman is the equal of a man any more than you can say that an apple is the equal of a peach. Courtship is a time to develop a taste for differences. How foolish are those engaged couples who spend their time of engagement in dissimulating their unique differences! There are young men who pretend to like dancing and bridge and avant garde poetry without any taste for such things at all. And there are young women, anxious to catch a man, who shiver through football games, suffer through the Friday night fights on TV, and listen with false avidity to a description of the inner workings of a hot-rod in order to prove that they are capable of adjustment in marriage. Courtship is the time to learn all the true, honest facets of personality of a future partner, not so much to discover whether one will be able to live with such interests, but whether one can honestly *promote* them! Love desires the fullest perfection of the beloved. Love, therefore, demands of the lover that he promote every potential strength of the partner in the unique manner in which he or she possesses those strengths.

Some people—young people, that is—often wonder what to do or talk about on a date. For two people truly in love, the longest courtship would not be enough to discover all the facets of the beloved's personality. Talking about the different interests should spark endless conversation. What are the future husband's ideals of social achievement? What kind of government would he like to see in his home town or state? What is his position on minimum wage laws, social security, the relations between the United States and Russia? What are the future wife's ideas about religious practices in their home, the nature of mother love, the effectiveness of different kinds of schooling, the relationships between home and school? What are his tastes in art and music? What are hers in literature and poetry? It should be a delightful discovery that each one is capable of indefinite self-revelation for a lifetime. How thrilling should be the possibility of mutual exploration for a lifetime together! Discovering and *loving* the different tastes of another and, in the loving, promoting them, is the root of true marital adjustment.

Chapter Four

COURTSHIP

WHAT IS TRUE LOVE?

Everyone knows and agrees that love is the basis of a happy marriage, but do we know what love is? Some people think love is a disease which one cannot avoid. You "catch" it. You recognize it just as clearly as you recognize a heavy cold. To such people thrills, hot and cold flashes, swooning sensations, and even a kind of fever are synonomous with love.

Certainly these romantic thrills are good and desirable. I suspect that some older married couples who laugh indulgently at the antics of young lovers are secretly a bit envious that, for them, these thrills have long since passed by. And yet deeply devoted spouses know that they are still in love even without the thrills. Again, many older couples entering marriage, though deeply devoted to each other, still do not experience this emotional frenzy.

Other people feel that love can be equivalent to the desire for—or ownership of—the beloved. A deeply spiritual man once confessed to me that, during his adolescence, in a desire to know what love was, he read every novel on love he could find. From this reading, he concluded that when two people violently desire to possess each other, they are in love. Yet, desire is an appetite for some external good. We *desire* ice cream or steak, the drunkard desires drink very avidly. Though it is true that an element of desire must exist in marriage, desire certainly is not the fullness of love. If it were, two people who were intensely jealous in their affection toward each other would be the world's greatest lovers. Yet everyone agrees that, although conjugal love is a kind of love exclusive of all others, jealousy is nevertheless a sign of immaturity in love. While a baby can well be jealous when he sees his mother giving affection to one of his older brothers or sisters, an older child should know that love is multiplied by being divided. An adult who is intensely jealous shows that his love has not risen much above the desire to possess or own his beloved.

True love is the ability and desire to promote the welfare of someone else. In this definition you will notice that there is no "I." The lover places the welfare of his beloved above his own; indeed, he makes that welfare his own welfare. He faces his beloved as another self. Another word for love is "devotion," which implies a dedication, a commitment, and a pledge of concern for the good of another.

We are devoted to our parents, our country, and our friends. When we are so devoted, we first of all *cultivate* such a love. I can hardly say I am devoted to my mother if I never visit her, never write to her, or never think of her. I must cultivate my love by keeping close to my mother, either physically or, at least, in spirit.

Secondly, when we are devoted, we *serve*. Service has fallen into bad repute in our country because Americans feel that it is a kind of slavery. Yet service is basic to true love. Notice how a mother will serve her children: she will scrub, dust, cook, mend, dry her children's tears, nurse them through illness, coax and cajole them, even punish them in order to better their behavior. A father, too, will serve. No longer does he spend his salary on himself; the needs of his wife and children are served first. He will worry and work to make each one of them contented and happy.

Thirdly, true love and devotion *support* the beloved. Support means to carry, to endure, to bear up, to act as a crutch. True lovers will "lend a hand" for every need.

A lover certainly will not allow his beloved to fall and hurt herself physically. And so lovers must support each other's emotional upsets, they must bear each other's faults, they must encourage each other to new efforts each day, they must be props to each other as each struggles to reach happiness, both in this life and in the next.

The devotion we have for our parents, our country, and our friends, is part-time devotion. Though we are devoted to our parents and visit them frequently, serve their needs through illness and old age, and give them of our substance as they need it, we all, sooner or later, leave the parental home to found our own families. Although we cultivate our love for our country, serve in the armed forces when necessary, support the government with our taxes, we are not concerned with devotion to country twenty-four hours a day. Friendships grow and wane. We keep in contact with our friends, we serve them occasional dinners, provide an evening of recreation. In disaster, we might well support them, too. But here, too, this cultivation and support is intermittent.

Conjugal love is this same intense devotion, full of constant cultivation, intense service, and full support, twenty-four hours a day throughout a lifetime. Indeed, married love, though similar to all other love, has a special quality because the young man and young woman love not only the person of their beloved but also a special conjugal unity which is achieved by their loving together. If a violin and a bow could speak, they would indicate that they need each other. But, though they are made for each other, they are made much more for the music that they bring forth. Married love has a quality which does not only fill out the mutual needs of a man and a woman, but also yearns implicitly for the creative achievement which makes a husband and wife a mother and father. Almost unconscious in the devotion of married love is the cultivation, service, and support of the one principle of generation which a man and woman make together. It is this principle of generation which not only brings a helpless infant into the world but also, by the constant exercise of the functions of mothering and fathering, brings that child to full maturity.

The three elements of romance, mutual desire, and deep devotion should all exist together in married love. But romance is like the breezes upon the stream—now a storm, now a ripple. Thrilling enthusiasm comes and goes. Desire can fade under boredom or grow to crushing possessiveness. Only the deep mutual devotion which is true married love can face the difficulties of a whole life together.

HOW LOVE GROWS

Have you ever thought how strange it is that two such different creatures as a little boy and a little girl could grow up to fall in love with each other? In the early years, boys and girls seem to be so utterly different as to be at war with each other. Little girls claim that little boys are rough and wild and little boys complain that little girls are silly and useless.

It is only in early adolescence that boys and girls suddenly become generally aware of each other. Up to this time they pointedly ignored each other. Now, confused and embarrassed by the new interest, they close ranks with other boys and girls in the same old gang they had a year or two before. But they cast longing looks toward the group of the opposite sex. Observe any group of fourteen- and fifteen-year-old boys and girls at a party. The boys gather in one corner of the room and the girls in the opposite corner. It is like pulling teeth to get them to pair up, even for a square dance. They protest and giggle that they can't dance or don't like a certain partner. But they are intensely aware of each other and the awareness, so new to them, makes them self-conscious.

This first general attraction between the sexes is the beginning of the long road toward true love between a man and a woman. It is discovering that there is another kind of human being with characteristics utterly different from one's own as masculine or feminine; it is a dawning wonder if the differences could possibly fill out one's own needs to be mature and complete.

Not many years later, adolescents go through an intense personal attraction to one other person. A girl will develop a "crush" on her "dream-man". It will matter little to her that her crew-cut swain is very gawky and tends to fall over his own feet. A boy will "carry a torch" for some shy young maiden. It will matter very little to him that her teeth are still in braces and that her saddle shoes are often not very clean. No one will ever convince him that she is not of the stuff that dreams are made of. Later, both of them will be very embarrassed at the memory of these mutual crushes. They will wonder what in the world was wrong with them and how they could have seen anything in each other at that early stage.

Yet this is an important time for growth. The adolescent boy and girl are really more in love with love than they are with each other. They cannot help yearning for the deep experience of true love and devotion, so they feel almost forced to discover what love is through "puppy love" affairs. The emotions are deep and real, but they are not solidly founded. Unfortunately many of our modern teenagers are so convinced that this is conjugal love that they insist on running off into marriage. They do not realize that adolescent love affairs are mostly emotional "play-acting" at love. Someone has said that the posturings of an adolescent are only an attempt to try on successive false faces until he finds one that fits his personality. I think that adolescent love affairs are very similar. They are constant attempts to try on the various aspects of love until there is the discovery of true love.

It is most unwise to recall all one's adolescent loves when true love finally comes on the scene. Young couples preparing for marriage frequently ask each other, "Am I the only one you have ever loved?" How foolish! You should be most happy that your beloved has gone through several adolescent crushes in his or her growing up. Perhaps only by numerous such experiences can he or she be certain that the present experience is the "real thing."

Other young couples, in the enthusiasm of their love, tell each other all about their earlier love affairs. Sometimes this causes intense jealousies and even bickerings which make the road of love far from smooth. Such confidences are just as foolish as demanding the protestation that "You are the only one I have ever loved."

After numerous experiences at adolescent emotional levels, a young man or woman is ready for true conjugal love. Sometimes this love comes in with all the enthusiasm of the earlier crush, but sometimes it grows quietly and calmly. But no matter how it comes, it must ultimately be based upon the calm determination to throw oneself away on one's beloved. It is a vow to dedicate oneself for a lifetime to the happiness of another person. Though all lovers should take careful aim before they throw themselves away, calculating carefully their own abilities and the potential of their beloved, married love has all the thrill of a gamble against long odds when the chips are down. Two people who wish to be married must take up the dice of life with deep determination and gamble on a lifetime together until death parts them. Only when they are willing to do this with clear-eyed vision of the sacrifices entailed can they say that they have grown up to adult love.

HOW TO DATE

The opposition of the Church to *too early* steady dating gives the impression that Catholics oppose steady dating always and at all times. This is not so. The Church is very much concerned that the young couple should go steady in preparation for marriage. After the joyous experience of growing up among one's peers, boys and girls tend to start to "shop around" for a possible marriage partner as they approach maturity. Somewhere in the early twenties, steady dating is a very important development in life. After shopping about for possibilities, a young man or woman will tend to go steady with one person for quite a long period, perhaps as long as six or ten months. The purpose of this steady, exclusive dating is to decide whether a proposal for an engagement and eventual marriage is in order for the couple. Once a man (or a woman) discovers that he has no interest in marriage with a steady partner, he should be adult enough to close off the relationship—there certainly is no future in it. Too many young people are hesitant to do this for fear of hurting the other. Yet, it certainly would be a much more serious injury to lead a dating partner on in hopes of a future marriage without having any intention of coming to the point of marriage.

When you are ready for marriage, it is important to follow common sense in your steady dating. By all means try to observe your dating partner in his or her natural habitat. Dating which enables one to observe a partner only in the romantic atmosphere of a night club, a movie, or in a car on a moon-lit night, will never give an understanding of that person. It is important to observe a young man or a young woman in his or her home.

Discover how your future husband treats his mother and his father, his brothers and his sisters. Is he kind and considerate to them, or is he irascible and distant? Is he too dependent upon his mother or father? Is he selfish with them? As he treats his nearest and dearest in kinship, he will tend to treat his own wife and children.

Observe, too, what kind of people comprise the family of your beloved. What are their customs? Have they held what, to you, seem strange and foreign ideas? Are they brusque with each other, or "great kidders"? Are they extremely polite and considerate? Do they make a great deal of the social graces? It is not a question here of judging whether or not they are the kind of people you *like*; it is a question of discovering whether or not you will be able to adjust to the kind of people they *are*. Your future husband or wife will tend to have the same general temperament and qualifications as those possessed by members of the family from which he or she comes. Romance may polish up the personality of your betrothed so that you cannot discover what he or she really is like, but your betrothed has a family who are not in love with you. They will be simple and natural and give you an idea about what he or she is.

More important is constant conversation between a couple who are about to be married on the principles of life. Ask yourself what you know about these principles. It is no good to ask these questions directly, because the moment's love may color the answer. It is better to carry on conversations and to discover indirectly the principles upon which your beloved bases his life. What does he think about divorce in general? Or about contraception? What are her convictions on religion in the home and religious practices? What kinds of material things are important to him, and which are relatively unimportant? What is her attitude on bearing children? His on child discipline? Is he a miser? Is she a spendthrift?

Discover now, during your steady dating period, your mutual interests. Do you enjoy talking things over together? This talking does not mean that two people should agree on everything, but it should mean that they find each other's views interesting. Politics, reading, music, sport, types of recreation, hobby interests, religious and vocational enthusiasms, personal observations of friends and relatives—all these things should form a constant series of conversations which will lead these two people to know each other better.

Steady dating also gives the two people the opportunity to discover whether they are physically attracted to each other. This does not give them any right to sinful intimacies. On the other hand, a young woman who shrinks from a kiss or embrace from her beloved certainly should not enter into marriage. After all, a normal anticipation of the joys of love-making together is a good natural appetite which should not be lacking in Christian marriage.

Lastly, steady dating is a time for sharing dreams together—dreams of love, of children, of success in the business world, of family happiness, of social impact, and of heaven together for all eternity.

As you consider all the things that should concern you while you are dating "steady," you will never need to wonder "what to do on a date." Time will be all too short as you work together towards the great day when you will walk down the aisle to the strains of the wedding march— and walk out again to achieve your destiny in a Christian marriage.

GOING STEADY

There is a great deal written in Catholic circles about "going steady." By "going steady," Catholic writers generally mean the frequent association of one boy with one girl, usually alone and in romantic situations, for the purpose of getting to know each other with a view to marriage. All Catholics know that the Church is opposed to this "going steady" for children in the grammar school grades and for high school students. The reasons are very serious and very important. We are opposed to steady dating at this time in life because the exclusive association of a boy and girl then is fraught with the danger of sins against purity. You cannot put a boy and girl together frequently and alone without causing passionate explosions. This is the result of original sin.

Yet, there are many other reasons against too early steady dating. Teenaged steady daters get hurt, first, because steady dating usually stops or at least retards emotional growth. The very young child is selfish by nature.

It doesn't care whether mother or dad are inconvenienced. Whenever it is hungry or wet, it will cry to have its needs met. The whole process of growth is to teach this child how to put himself second. Gradually through a lifetime a baby must learn to share with others and eventually to dedicate himself to the service of others. Maturity is the measure of the ability of someone to love another for himself. One must be full of love before he can give that love to another.

Dating with different girls and boys in early adolescence is a wonderful opportunity to get to know others, to begin to experience what a man is and what a woman is, but this early dating is still for self-growth, not for self-giving. Adolescence is a time designed by God to enable the growing boy or girl to develop fully in every way—body, emotions, mind, and heart—so that they have something worthwhile to give when they fall in love. When they start to give affection in steady dating, they are emptying themselves before they are full. When a farmer has dug a well, he does not immediately start pumping. He lets the well fill first. Otherwise his demand will always be ahead of his supply.

Ask any teenager why he or she dates steadily. Is it because they really like the other person? Or is it more that they like what they are *getting out* of the relationship. The steady dater wants to make sure that she has a dancing partner for all dances. The boy may want to get approval from his gang. Isn't this selfish? Isn't this an attempt to bolster up one's own ego? If this is true, then love is not the reason, because love is concerned with the growth and development of *another*.

As a prelude to marriage, steady dating, and eventual engagement, are proper and right because steady dating is a method of learning how to give in love. On the other hand, steady dating in adolescence is a method of exploiting a partner—a method of increasing one's selfishness. It is a kind of adolescent social security—a security that is bolstered up by someone else. Though at first sight this security seems very helpful, since it is important for young people to find security, in the long run it is very disastrous. Security should flow from the conviction of one's loveableness in himself, and the willingness to love another for herself. Security cannot safely come from anxious desire to artificially bolster up one's sense of attractiveness by tying someone to exclusive dating.

Teenagers who go into steady dating also harm themselves, sooner or later, by becoming emotionally involved. I am not speaking here of sins of passion but simply of the emotional attachment two people develop who like each other very much. However much they may protest that they do not mean to *own* each other, they cannot help developing an emotional need for the other. As soon as the steady date looks at another person, pangs of jealousy arise. If one decides to break up, the break-up may precipitate a heart-rending situation even when they have agreed beforehand, "Whenever you say, I'll go my way and you yours." Separation still hurts. One is sure to get hurt.

Sometimes, even worse, is the turmoil of the steady dater who would prefer to break up but who doesn't want to hurt the other person. To be bound by promise to someone to whom one is no longer attracted is certainly a harmful experience. Someone is bound to get hurt!

Steady dating, while it seems to slow up the maturing of an individual also accelerates the age of marriage. Boys and girls are marrying today at an age earlier than ever before. Many young people are married within a few months after high school graduation. Though youthfulness can be an ally to adjustment in marriage, steady dating has often slowed down maturing processes, and as a result brings two emotional children together. It is a statistical fact that there is a far greater break-up in marriage, whether by divorce or separation, in those couples who marry before twenty than in those who marry after that age. *Somebody is bound to get hurt.*

Let's face it. Steady dating also leads to frequent sins

of impurity. Even if a boy and girl do not know what love really is, their romantic enthusiasm makes them believe that they do know. Love indeed tends toward unity. A mother crushes her child to her breast. Lovers wish to kiss and embrace, but kissing and embracing are only paths to the road that leads to complete bodily union reserved for the holiness of matrimony. Young people who start too early on the path will find themselves too soon on the road and will quickly burden themselves with the weight of many mortal sins. *Somebody is bound to get hurt.*

Steady daters in teenage make poor students. Ask any teacher which pupils show greatest loss of interest in study and self-development, and she will tell you "the love birds." The moaning and moping that goes with romantic love has been caricatured and lampooned too often to need further discussion. If a student suddenly loses interest in study due to romantic passion, he will not develop his mind. Many youngsters foolishly discontinue their education and rush off into marriage. They will look back with regret to the lost years when they face the possibility of an advance in work that depends entirely upon the level of their education. *Somebody is bound to get hurt.*

Teenagers frequently use the argument, "Everybody's doing it," or even, "My best friend Mary is doing it." Perhaps not one of the teenagers really wants to date this way, but it started and they don't know how to stop. Group action with full understanding of parental objections and teenagers' needs will bring a solution in your area.

WHAT IS CHASTITY?

Sobriety does not mean the absence of drunkenness. Such a notion would make of sobriety merely a negative virtue. Nor does it mean never taking a drink, or worse, despising drink. Again, sobriety does not mean a lack of taste for alcoholic beverages. Sobriety means the joyous control and direction of the appetite for alcohol.

The puritan who rejects all drink is rejecting a gift of God. A man who has no taste for drink simply lacks sensibility, which is a defect in his nature. The person who merely avoids the ultimate excess which is drunkenness does no more than avoid sin. The Christian who enjoys drink as a gift of God, but neither drools at the thought of liquor nor fears and hates it, practices Christian sobriety.

In a similar fashion, chastity is a positive, not a negative, virtue. The mere avoidance of serious sins against this virtue is not true chastity. Lack of attraction to the gift of self in the marriage embrace is insensibility to a very real value which God has given to men and women to be used according to God's law within marriage. To equate chastity and virginity, as many people do, is to misunderstand the virtue altogether.

Confusion about chastity arises from our strong instinctual natures which tend too easily toward sin—in this area above all others. The struggle for self-control is hard. Falls may be frequent. Weariness in the battle makes many people reject the very value they fight to achieve. Sometimes preaching inveighs so strongly against impurity that many of us absorb an unconscious impression that physical love is always and at all times wrong, but, somehow or other, "justified" within marriage—as though marriage gave some sort of license for lust.

Chastity is a positive virtue. It is a virtue which *controls* and *directs* the expression of physical love according to God's law. Since God's law indicates that this type of love expression must be a total self-dedication for a lifetime to one person of the other sex, and that it must be used towards the procreation and education of children, such complete bodily self-giving may be used only within the holiness of valid marriage. Chastity, therefore, means the non-expression of complete physical love outside of marriage and the gift of self within marriage only according to the law of God. Physical love, therefore, is not an evil thing somehow justified by a marriage contract but an experience so good and noble that it is wrong and sinful to seek it outside of marriage. It is wrong to suggest or imagine that a man and a woman living a Christian married life have lost their chastity. If this were so, Pope Pius XI could not have entitled his famous encyclical on marriage, "On *Chaste* Wedlock."

It should be clear that chastity is a virtue which must be practiced positively for an entire lifetime. It is *one* virtue with *two* different sets of practical applications. One concrete set of applications applies to those who are not married, and another applies to those who are. Yet, despite the difference of concrete application, it is one indivisible virtue.

This has very important repercussions which many young people do not understand. A boy or a girl who does not live a perfectly chaste life during adolescence, dating, and courtship will find it difficult to live chastely under God's law in marriage. One cannot learn to practice a virtue in the future by refusing to practice that same virtue in the present. A young person who sins, constantly and habitually, alone or with others, will find marriage no solution to the problem of personal purity. Chastity cannot be learned from unchastity.

Many people profess not to understand how this can be so; yet it is as psychologically clear as it is logically clear. A young man or a young woman who has never bothered to learn self-control before marriage will not learn it in marriage; and self-control is necessary in marriage, contrary to the opinion of many today. A young man or young woman who has been sinfully free with the body, distributing impure caresses and receiving them wherever they could be found, will not find fidelity to marriage easy. The abstinence demanded by a spouse's illness, by the complications of pregnancy, or by the advice of a doctor will not be achieved by the young spouses who have never learned to control and direct their appetites. Finally, the temptation to contraception in marriage is strong in an intemperate husband or wife.

Does this mean that anyone guilty of impurity during adolescence is automatically doomed to unchastity in marriage? Certainly not! Thanks to the grace of God we can all change our ways. The stories of the many great converts in the history of the Church—St. Mary Magdalene and St. Augustine, for example—show that great sanctity is not precluded by sin or even by the habit of sin. With God's grace, it is always possible to rebuild a life. Young people, then, who are truly sorry for past lapses and who work hard on the virtue can hope with certainty that God will give them the graces they need to live a successful and chaste marriage. But if there is no attempt to correct one's life, disaster is inevitable.

All the laws in the world come, directly or indirectly, from God. The natural laws which govern such things as falling bodies and atomic fission come from the same God who makes the law of chastity. No one ever truly succeeds in *breaking* one of God's laws. We may attempt to violate the law, but it is not the law we break—we break or harm ourselves! A person who, in defiance of the law of gravity, walks out a second story window does not break the law of gravity; the law of gravity breaks him. A person who violates the law of sobriety harms himself; he is not only punished in the next life, but he pays in this life by harming himself with a hangover, physical harm, and mental disgust.

In the same way, the person who violates the law of chastity does not break the law; the law breaks him. Though the consequences of unchastity are not so apparent as the hangover after a drunken spree, they are, nevertheless, as real. Unchastity brands its devotee as an immature person, as one who probably cannot be depended upon for permanent love. Sins of impurity, by filling the imagination with lustful images, enervate mental processes, make study difficult, and even convince the practitioner that he is not a free captain of his fate but a slave fettered by appetite. Though impurity does not cause physical disease, it brings on a kind of hopeless lassitude. Without doubt, unchastity marks the whole personality and mentality of its practitioners.

Since all the laws of God in the moral area direct the love of a human being in the direction for which God has designed it, no one could ever blame true love for unchastity. No one could truly say: "We're in love, so we can't help unchastity." Unchastity marks a person as one who cannot love as God wishes him to. Since human love is but a *reflection* of divine love, to destroy divine love in one's own and the beloved's soul is also to destroy human love. Impurity says to its partner: "I hate you, I care not for your eternity in Hell." Pre-marital chastity is therefore necessary for love during courtship, and marital chastity is equally necessary for married love. Both are but two aspects of the one virtue of positive love.

Chapter Five

THE VOCATION

MARRIAGE IS A SUBLIME VOCATION

Everyone has a vocation. We usually think of a vocation as a voice calling us, but there are many other ways of understanding it. A vocation or calling can be understood as an impulse and, in this sense, each one of us is called out of nothingness. God can be imitated in literally an infinite number of ways. As He looks at all these possible ways, He gives a nod, an impulse, a call into existence. This was how the world was formed, as were the myriads of flowers and the richness of the varied universe. Each blade of grass, each leaf on a tree, each furry animal, has some little facet to reflect God.

In a much higher way, God has called each human being into existence. Though all the plants and animals are similar to their own species, a human being has both similarity and uniqueness. It is said that God breaks the mold into which He casts each new soul. Each yearning in a human being finds its source in a need to reflect God in some way, to answer the call that God gave when He created that human soul.

The call of God is not only exerted by the very fact of a man's existence but also by the kind of a personality he is, the circumstances in which he finds himself, or the impact of hard reality which cannot be changed. We say of certain people that they have a natural bent towards music or mathematics. Such a natural inclination indicates that it could well be that God is calling such a person to a par-

ticular social service revolving about their talent. The
majority of the human race have a natural inclination
towards marriage in general. Unless some intervening
grace comes along to change this inclination from marriage to celibacy, we must recognize that the inclination
to marriage is an indication that the state of matrimony
is the vocation of the individual.

Again, circumstances place a man and a woman in close
proximity; they work together, travel together on the
same bus, meet at some social affair, bump into each other
in a corridor. Friendship springs up and the natural inclination towards marriage centers about this one particular person. While always leaving room for freedom of
human choice, circumstances frequently indicate the vocation from God to enter into marriage with this one
particular person. Finally, the impact of some hard facts
may change both natural inclinations and general circumstances: debilitating illness, economic poverty, obligations
to family, dedication to some special kind of service, might
preclude marriage.

Natural inclination, circumstances, and the facts of existence, permit—and frequently lead—men and women
into marriage. At the base of the natural inclination is
the natural inward yearning for the experience of married love. The code of Church law coldly defines marriage
as the contract which gives to each partner the right to
the body of his or her partner for actions which tend towards the generation of a child. Founded upon this good
and noble impulse is the desire to set up a home together
and to see the children through their entire education to
Christian maturity. It leads the couple to be willing to
divide up the labor of bearing, rearing, and supporting
children; it leads them to bear each other's weaknesses,
to support each other in love. This is the root of the spiritual calling of marriage.

Just as one called to the priesthood has a natural inclination to serve the community, a special call from God in terms of special graces, and a unique sacrament which consecrates him and enables him to perform his function in saying Mass, hearing confessions, baptizing infants, anointing the aged and ill; so those called to marriage have the natural desire or inclination to serve their beloved and their children. They have, from this natural inclination, a call or vocation. They, too, have a special sacrament which consecrates their love in Christian marriage and enables them to perform their special duties. In so doing, they are called to fill out the needs of the temporal community, to spread the human race throughout the earth, to extend the Mystical Body of Christ, to fill the earth with other adorers of God, and to people heaven with saints. Truly, this is a real vocation, a special spiritual calling for a special kind of supernatural service.

Married people are also called to share in the very power of God. They share in the power of God's creation. Though it is true that only God can truly create, and though it is equally true that He could have called each person into existence directly and immediately by His own power, He wills to share that power with human parents. Their expression of love is called procreation, a beautifully expressive term which tells us that parents are to create for, by, with, and in God.

Parents also share the providence of God. The providence of God is a matter of bringing into effect the plan which God has for all eternity. The material world of rocks and rivers, the plant world of plant and tree, the animal world of fishes and birds, God brings to the fullness of His plan by laws planted in these things. All things have the appetite to answer their own call. Gravity explains the appetite of material things to reach their center, plants struggle up from the earth to reach the sun, animals are born, grow, mate, and die according to an inner set of instincts. To human beings, however, God gives the privilege of sharing His own plan and its execution through their intelligence. Though God cares for the birds in the air directly, and manages the seasons without our help, He hands over the spiritual and physical development of husband to wife and wife to husband, and He gives to both of them a family of children to raise to Christian maturity for Him. It is parents above all who share in the planning of God for the fulfillment of His design for the world.

Husband and wife also share in Christ's power. By the sacrament of matrimony, they receive special spiritual powers over each other and over their children. They try to apply the redemption of Christ in sanctifying themselves, each other, and their children. They take over, also, His function as teacher, in that it is through parents that children learn what is the Fatherhood of God, the Motherhood of our Lady, the nature of divine providence, the end and purpose of life. Finally, they share in Christ's power as King. Christ said, "All power in heaven and on earth has been given to me" (Matt. 28:18). Since all power on earth comes from Christ, the authority which husband has over wife and parents over their children is the authority of Christ. This is especially clear when we realize that a valid marriage between two baptized Christians recreates in miniature the very union of Christ with His Church.

Marriage is truly a sublime vocation.

ARE MARRIAGES MADE IN HEAVEN?

Human beings contract a marriage, and probably most people could be happy with any one of a hundred possible partners. But once two baptized persons contract a valid marriage, this marriage is truly ratified and constituted in heaven because the valid marriage of two baptized people is a sacrament.

Christ redeemed all men some 1900 years ago. Not only did He buy them back from slavery to evil by His blood, but He also raised them to a divine level. He won sanctifying grace for them. By way of analogy sanctifying grace is to the soul what electricity is to a light bulb. Just as electricity transforms the filaments and glass and makes them something more than they are by nature, so sanctifying grace transforms a human being and makes him participate in the life of God. We can truly say that sanctifying grace *divinizes* a man.

There are seven contact points through which a person can be electrified—divinized—with the life of God called grace. He is born to divine life by Baptism. He matures in this life through Confirmation. He is nourished divinely by the Body and Blood of Christ. When this life is asphyxiated by sin, Penance can resuscitate it. Divine life is brought to eternal fulness with Extreme Unction. A man may be divinized as a special mediator before God with Holy Orders. A man and woman catch up the love-life of God in the sacrament of Matrimony.

Marriage as a sacrament makes the union of husband and wife a divine thing. Each is supernaturalized as lover and beloved. No longer is their love the weak human thing it was, full of the possibility of loss and boredom and weariness. Now it has the depth, the eternity, the power, the finality of divinity itself.

The sacrament of Matrimony further makes human conjugal union a miniature of the Mystical Body of Christ. No longer is a man a husband and father, he is Christ loving His Church. No longer is a woman merely a wife and mother, she becomes a spouse to Christ. St. Paul says, "Let wives be subject to their husbands as to the Lord; because a husband is head of the wife, just as Christ is head of the Church. Husbands, love your wives, just as Christ also loved the Church, and delivered Himself up for her. Even thus ought husbands also to love their wives as their own bodies. For no one ever hated his own flesh; on the contrary he nourishes and cherishes it, as Christ also does the Church" (Eph. 5: 23-29).

God the Father can never abandon His own Son, for He and the Son are of one nature. Christ can never forget the Church, for He is of one flesh with her. So also God can never abandon a Christian married couple, since they are living His own life and love. Therefore, along with their divinized union, they have the right to all the helps and inspirations they need to live this divine plan of marriage. When it is time to apologize, to forgive, to encourage, to meet a partner's need, to face economic pressures, those who have the sacrament of Matrimony can know that they have only to "ask and they shall receive" all the help they need.

There is more. The sacrament gives not only helps, but remedies. All the sins against marriage and each other, all the failures, all the little and big infidelities, all the weak surrenders to human frailty can be remedied. They can fade as so many evil dreams if a Christian wife or husband will stir up the grace that is in them.

Though weddings are made on earth, Christian marriage is ratified and made divine in heaven.

TWO IN ONE FLESH

In the very first pages of the Old Testament, Adam described marriage: ". . . For this cause a man shall leave home and father and mother and cleave to his wife and they shall become two in one flesh" (Gen. 2: 24). In the New Testament, Our Lord Himself continued this description of marriage when He added, ". . . Therefore they are now no longer two but one flesh..." (Mark 10: 8). Though we are naturally reticent about this basic fact of marriage, it is an open secret that marriage revolves about a mutual, total self-dedication, a self-gift of body and soul which is called marital union or the marital act. It is this

union of bodies which is the material of the marriage contract. The Church's canon law defines marriage as a contract which gives to each partner the right to the body of
his partner for actions which tend toward the generation
of a child. Cold, legal language, indeed! Yet this cold definition describes the sacred reality raised to a supernatural
level by the sacrament of Matrimony.

In all the cultures of the world we find a sense of religious awe and respectful reticence at this mysterious union. Yet regularly in history there have been attempts to
be "frank" about the mystery and to "debunk" it. Clinical
terminology has been adopted in our modern times and
"enlightened" people are presumed able to speak about
this inscrutable reality in an utterly unemotional atmosphere. Rather than take the mystery out of sex however,
we need to retain it.

If the word "mysterious" applied to the marriage union
means a shameful, shocking secret which had better be
left unknown, then we should eliminate the mystery. But
if "mysterious" means a reality beyond description, the
meaning of which cannot be fully grasped; if it means a
reality which demands religious reverence akin to that
with which Moses approached the Burning Bush; if it
points out a means of communication between a man and
woman which cannot be achieved by words or gestures;
if it refers to cooperation with God in "filling the earth
with adorers of God and peopling Heaven with saints"
(St. Francis de Sales) ; then by all means let us keep the
mystery in sex. "Scientific" description will give only the
kind of knowledge a person can obtain by finding out that
Michelangelo's "Moses" contains so many tons of marble
and took so many weeks to complete.

Whenever this subject is not deeply and reverently understood, we find many false notions in people's minds.
Some people have the idea that the body is evil and that
the marital relation is an evil act which is permitted
within legitimate marriage only as a concession to poor

weak human nature. Others, using Victorian thinking, try to pretend that there is no body. At the very least, they think that they will be happier if they ignore the body. On the other hand, pagans, both ancient and modern, think of the marital relation merely as a form of play, a method of having an intense kind of physical fun very similar to the pleasure in eating or drinking.

Many Christians have unconsciously absorbed one or other of these approaches. Since we are all involved in the struggle to control and direct this powerful appetite, it is easy to drift into a conviction that the marital union is always and at all times wrong but somehow or other "blessed" in marriage. We sometimes imply that the sacrament of Matrimony consecrates the marital union in a fashion similar to the way in which clothing and make-up artfully conceal a homely body and physical features.

The true Christian approach to the marital act is one of awe at a reality sacred in itself. How it is possible for two people, a man and a woman, to communicate with each other so deeply and intimately and, in the communication, to cooperate with God in the procreation of a child, is a mysterious and never-to-be-understood fact. No amount of scientific frankness will help the human being to enter any more deeply into the mystery.

Bodily love is not something basically wrong, somehow justified in marriage, but the other way around. It is so mysterious, so holy, so demanding of permanence, that there must be a state—the married state—in which its sacredness is protected. The reason why its use is forbidden outside of marriage is the sacredness of marriage itself. A Christian married couple must approach the marriage act with a reverence similar to that with which a human being approaches the handling of the Blessed Sacrament. Only a consecrated person—a priest—may touch the sacred species; only a consecrated couple may approach the marital embrace.

The approach to the love experience of marriage is different in men and women. A man tends to approach the experience on a more physical, pleasurable level. A woman is concerned with the meaning of her total gift of self within the act. Both must learn from each other. Both pleasure and meaning are important. Hence, the husband must learn the meaning of physical affection on an emotional and spiritual level and a wife must learn not to reject the sensible passion which God himself has created as a real value in human lovelife.

Negative emotions will spoil marriage unity. Fear is the main enemy of success. Whether this fear be of a possible child, of committing sin through the physical expression of love (when this expression is misunderstood), the results may be damaging to a marriage. Another danger in this regard is emotional fatigue and discouragement. Two people who are weary of life and its frustrations will hardly be concerned about the needs of each other. They will sink into selfish self-pity that their life is not more easy and successful. They will use their union merely to sate their own selfish physical needs.

Love is essentially a concern for the well-being of a partner. Only if a husband and wife are concerned for each other's needs in all areas, and reflect this concern for each other in the marital embrace, will they achieve a satisfactory physical relationship. Techniques can be of value only in the service of love. Once the married couple realizes that the marital embrace is not a mere physical action but a language of achieving oneness of mind, heart, and affection, they will easily discover their own physical language of love. Without such an awareness, techniques can only become a series of methods of mutual exploitation and will engender not real unity but boredom, rejection, and disgust.

The young couple preparing for marriage should face with clear eyes and clear head the reality of two-in-one-flesh. It would be unrealistic and foolish to ignore this basic reality upon which the contract of Holy Matrimony is founded. What God Himself has created must be accepted with reverence. On the other hand, it would be equally dangerous to approach this reality with pagan avidity because, though physical love is the basic reality upon which marriage is built, it is not the be-all or end-all of married existence.

THE MYSTERY OF MARRIAGE

Love is at the basis of all zest for living. It is love which sends the young virgin joyfully to the convent; it is love which makes the doctor and the nurse attend the most contagious—or even the most disgusting—diseases. It is love which makes the priest chase after his lost sheep, even when they run from his attentions and return only hatred for service. It is love which sends the young couple off with swinging step to found a new life together, confident that no difficulty will be too great to surmount. But what is love? Though we can say that love is at the basis of life, we can understand life much more easily than we can understand love. Love, even in the human sense, is a mysterious reality, but once consecrated and divinized by the sacrament of matrimony, it becomes not only a mysterious but a mystical reality.

God has always chosen the love of husband and wife to explain the most deep and intimate unions that He has ever entered into with human nature. Indeed, He always calls His unity marriage. Look through the Old Testament and discover God's concern for His chosen people. Throughout the Old Testament, there is never a word which describes the defections of the chosen people from their devotion to God in terms of infidelity, heresy, or schism. The inspired writers have always pointed out that, in pursuing false gods and leaving their own true God behind, they were fornicators or adulterers. Again and again in the Old Testament you will find the combination, "an evil and adulterous generation." In the Old Testament, God is always pictured as a loving husband, the chosen people as a spouse or wife, however erring. How mysterious that God should have chosen nuptial love to explain His deep union with His chosen people.

Many people have wondered about the Canticle of Canticles in the Old Testament. At the first reading, it seems to be an erotic poem. It always has been a mysterious book for the commentators. The best interpretation seems to be that it is a play in which the young bride has been stolen away from her young husband, the shepherd, and placed in the harem of an eastern king. The entire poem concerns the yearning of the wife for the husband and the husband for the wife. God has written this through the inspired writer to show His yearning for His chosen people and the chosen people for Him.

This poetic effusion of the Old Testament has been used by every one of the saintly mystics to explain their deep union with God in the ecstatic experience. In their visions and mystical unities with God, almost all the saints have described their union as a marriage union. You may have seen the painting of the wedding of St. Catherine which points out a virginal "marriage" with Christ. Even the shy and almost Victorian St. Therese of the Child Jesus boldly selects passages from the Canticle of Canticles to express her deep love for God.

We have already pointed out how St. Paul described the unity of Christ with His Church as a wedded union. We speak constantly of Holy Mother the Church, the Spouse of Christ. The word "spouse," of course, means wife. How sublime that human marriage should be described in terms of Christ's unity with the Church and Christ's unity with the Church in terms of human marriage. Certainly no base or ignoble union could be predicated of human marriage when St. Paul could indicate that marriage is not only a symbol, but a reliving of the unity of Christ and His Church. When he says, "Let wives be subject to their husbands as to the Lord; . . . Husbands, love your wives, just as Christ also loved the Church," (Ephesians 5: 22 and 25) he presents us with an endless wondering source of meditation on the mysterious reality of nuptial love.

Finally, many saints speak of the wedding of the human and divine nature in Christ. Here is a marriage that defies all description because the incarnation—the enfleshing—of the second person of the Trinity in human flesh defies all understanding.

Really, we should speak of five different marriages. We can meditate long and wonderingly on the marriage of the human and divine natures in Christ. We can stand in awe at the unity of God and His chosen people so frequently described in the Old Testament. The wedding of God and a chosen soul in the ecstasies of mystical experiences given to a St. Francis of Assisi, a St. Teresa, and thousands of others almost overwhelms us. The nuptial love of Christ for His Church and the Church for Christ is such a bold concept that it almost shocks us. The supernatural unity of a Christian marriage, though the least example of married unity, still defies full human understanding. Yes, here are five real marriages, each uniquely different from the other yet each a reflection of all of the others.

The mystery of married love will never be understood by human minds until we all shall meditate upon it together in Heaven when we shall achieve a wedded unity with God Himself forever.

Chapter Six

MARRIED LOVE

LOVE IS EXCLUSIVE

One of the most remarkable qualities of married love is its exclusiveness. No other human love has this quality. Only an immature child, indeed, a baby, would be concerned that his parents are loved by their other children. All of us have many friends and love them dearly. When we love God deeply and intensely, though we place Him first in our affections (as we should do), it does not disturb us that there are others who love Him, and, in the case of the great saints, love Him more than we do. We go so far as to want everyone to love Him.

Conjugal love, however, is different. Although the lover may want to tell the whole world that he is in love, although he may want people to appreciate how loveable his beloved is, he can never desire that she give her love, in a married fashion, to anyone other than himself. He will be anxious that she continue to love all her own friends. He will wish her to be close to God in deepest sanctity. He will not be jealous of the love she gives her parents. But, he will want the special love which is that of a wife only for himself. He will wish to give to her, as to no other, his love as husband.

This is because husband and wife, in achieving married unity, achieve something that is greater than either of them alone and greater than the sum of their two complete personalities. In mathematics, one plus one equals two; but, in marriage, one plus one equals *one*! This oneness or unity has a unique value. Not only does it fill out the deficiencies of each sex by the strengths of the other, it also creates a single principle of generation and education. It results in a special unity called a family. Christ Himself said, "They shall become two in one flesh." This two-in-oneness is a special reality, a mysterious existence which demands that married love be exclusive of all others.

The love upon which two build their marriage must also be *perpetual*. Every poet, every singer of love songs, has dwelt upon this quality of eternity in love. Can you imagine a young lover saying to his beloved, "Let's fall in love for two and a half years"? No, he protests over and over again that his love is "forever"; that it will continue "until the end of time"; and that "I can't stop loving you!"

It is no mere accident or social custom that demands conjugal love to be pledged "until death." No matter how pagan the world in which we live, love yearns to vow a lifetime of love. Even in a land which condones the most shocking divorce and separation rate, hardly anyone has thought to change the ritual of marriage to any other words than those indicating a lifetime of mutual dedication.

The perpetuity of wedded love is one of the reasons why it is so gravely sinful to give one's body to another outside the state of wedlock. This gift of self, whether it be the total gift, or even the lesser exchanges of intimate affection, is the method of symbolizing and achieving perpetual love. Marriage union is the total surrender of self without the possibility of ever asking that self back. One can never offer such a perpetual gift just for the moment, or only temporarily. To do so would be to sin against the very nature of wedded love itself. Ask any thoughtful person who has "gone too far," and he or she will tell you that the psychological effect of impurity is to tear the spirit asunder as one tries to give and not give, to make this perpetual gift on a part-time basis.

The old English term for marriage is "wedlock." Think for a moment what the word means: a mutual chaining together. It means that a man and a woman are locked in each other's hearts and minds forever. And although a cynical world may crack jokes about a man and woman being "a ball and chain" for each other, though the world may smile pityingly at the mutual loss of freedom, lovers know in their hearts it must be so. Have you ever noticed dandelion seeds floating freely in the air? They seem to be free, yet their whole being demands that they be rooted in, chained to the earth. Only in this way can they come to flower. Love can be perfected only when the lover is locked to his beloved forever.

Pope Pius XII made perpetuity of married love even more thrilling when, in his sermon to widows, he pointed out that though marriage, in its juridical effects, ceases upon the death of either partner, "conjugal love with all its splendor and its eternal vows, lives on just as the spiritual and free beings live on who have pledged themselves to each other."

Ask yourself, then, do I desire my beloved above, and exclusive of, all others? Do I want her to love me alone? Do I want our love to last until the end of time? If you can answer, yes, with a deep awareness of what these questions mean and what sacrifices they may entail when the enthusiasm of romance has faded, you have found another set of characteristics for the love necessary for marital happiness.

LOVE IS SERVICE

A most important characteristic of the love upon which a happy and successful marriage may be built is that of *unselfishness*. Notice that I have not said that married love must be selfless. Since each one of us is imperfect, we must, by nature, seek after the development of which we are capable. When two people fall in love, they inevitably see in each other possible fulfillments of their own needs. The very differences between a man and a woman are the things that draw them together, like charges of positive and negative electricity. Like the opposite poles of a magnet, they complement each other, each filling out the other's weaknesses with their strengths and, in turn, having their own weaknesses strengthened.

But this self-fulfillment in each other is a far cry from selfishness. Selfishness is irreverent, and does not respect the strengths of a partner. Selfish love does not want the other person to be any more than an appendage. It is a pride that wants to make over the partner into the other's own image and likeness. Selfish love is unwilling to admit weakness; it reduces a partner to a mere servant or slave. No matter how passionate and romantic the attraction, if a man corrects his future wife's taste in clothing, in jewelry, in food; if he cannot brook any disagreement or different point of view; his love for his partner is selfish and dangerous. Again, although every woman sees her mate's potential and hopes for him to develop it to the full, if she sees in her future married partner *only* a blob of masculinity to form according to her own pattern of what a man should be, if she nags at him constantly to attempt things beyond his ability, her love is selfish.

You have probably heard it said many times that marriage is a fifty-fifty proposition. A young man about to be married will tell the boys at work, "I know what I'm getting into. No one is going to shove me around. I'll only go half-way in marriage and she'll have to come the other half." Girls in their secretarial offices often say the same things, with the appropriate feminine variations. This is not unselfish love. Marriage demands of love 100 per cent self-dedication from both sides.

This should not be hard to see. If a husband or wife is only going to give fifty per cent of himself or herself to their marriage, then they will judge that percentage from their own point of view. How can you measure what is half-way in love? Love is a qualitative, not a quantitative, thing, and qualities cannot be measured with a yardstick. Again, what will happen to married love when one partner or the other is unable to contribute his or her share at the moment? There are times when a man is so weary, discouraged, and depressed, that he feels almost like suicide. His marriage and family obligations will occasionally weigh upon him like the world on Atlas. His wife will then need 100 per cent in patience. At other times, a woman will be ready to throw up, not only her breakfast, but also her marriage during the early days of pregnancy. On occasion, she will be almost willing to put her children "in a box, tie it with a ribbon, and drop it in the middle of the sea." Only a 100 per cent from her husband will win the day.

The strangest thing about 100 per cent self-dedication is that it is the only way to win complete happiness. In terms of love and happiness, we get only by giving. Christ Himself has taught us this very clearly. He says "He who gains his life loses it." In other words, he who doles out his love-service drop by drop, who says, "I'm getting mine; nobody is shoving me around," loses even the life which he so carefully treasures. Our Lord continues, "He who loses his life in this world, keeps it, even to life everlasting." In other words, Christ tells us that he who enthusiastically throws his life away in service, he who does not count the cost of living, achieves complete happiness in this life and, further, keeps that happiness right through to eternity. In explaining how this can be, our Lord says, "Unless the grain of wheat fall into the ground and die, it remains alone; but if it die, it brings forth fruit an hundred-fold."

Loneliness is certainly the greatest disaster for a lover and yet, if that lover preserves his own personality like a single grain of wheat, loneliness, unproductiveness, and unfruitfulness will be his. But if he allows his self to die as the grain of wheat seems to die when it is placed in the ground, his harvest of happiness is a hundredfold. Notice, our Lord seems to promise a ten thousand per cent return on the investment of total self-dedication.

We Catholics who have the Word of Life do not fully believe this promise of Christ; we are always counting the cost of dedication and never the rewards. And yet, it should not be so strange to us. Look back on your life as a child. When was your mother happiest? Did she really enjoy Mother's Day, when you pushed her out of the kitchen and insisted upon her reigning as queen in the parlor, wearing her best clothes and eating the candy you gave her to show your love? I suspect that she was much happier in those Christmas days when she had all the children and grandchildren in. Recall how she got up early in the morning in order to put the turkey in the oven. All morning long she worked in the kitchen, making sure that every bit of food was done to perfection. Remember how she called you all in to partake of the feast and perhaps only sat down herself to a few cold bites after the turkey had been reduced to a skeleton. Remember her face; you saw there the quiet happiness that comes from the forgetfulness of self in the service of those who are loved above all. This is where she found her self-fulfillment—in forgetting herself.

Here is the paradox of love. The love which brings us the greatest degree of happiness is the love which is totally dedicated to the happiness of another. Selfishness and love are contradictory. The lover finds his happiness in giving happiness to his beloved; indeed, he finds another self in his beloved, and her happiness and his happiness become one and the same. Before you risk marriage, ask yourself whether you are willing to lose yourself in service in order to gain love. Try to discover the same willingness in your partner. Compare your willingness for service with that of Christ, who, in the words of St. Paul, "though He was by nature God, did not consider being equal to God a thing to be clung to, but emptied Himself, taking the nature of a slave and being made like unto men."

LOVE IS TENDER

A quality of married love that engaged couples can anticipate, and look forward to preserving in their lives, is the *tenderness* of love. Under this quality of tenderness, all the wonderful emotional factors of romantic love fit in. We rarely feel emotional love for others, even for our parents. When we are young, we cling to our parents, of course, but this is more because we need love than because we wish to give it. All too soon we tend to take our parents for granted. Our closest friends are seldom the recipients of emotional love. We may confide our woes and our joys to them, but this has very little relation to the deep tenderness that married lovers can and should feel for each other.

This deep tenderness is given to the young wedded couple in order for them to build a lifetime of conjugal devotion. Romantic love is like the tinder we use to build a fire. Like the tinder, it flares up with intense, quick heat and almost sears with its intensity. Tinder builds the even heat we want in a room; romantic love is given to a couple to build the even climate of warm, permanent married love.

A warning is necessary here. Romantic love with all its tenderness will not continue with the same intensity throughout life. No one who is truly realistic could ever hope that it would. And yet many young married couples are constantly examining the tenderness of their love to see if it matches that which they felt when they first met.

Should they notice that the emotional fire is waning, they quickly panic and try to rush off together to find it again. How foolish! Trying to build marital love upon tenderness alone is like trying to keep a dark room lighted by striking successive matches. The flare-up is quick and bright, but it soon fades unless the flame is touched to the candle. In the same way, tenderness is important to start love, but it is not the love itself.

This is not to say that tenderness should be permitted to fade quickly from married life. Tenderness should always be there, but it will grow and wane and have different lights and shadows as life moves on. Now a shared sorrow, now a quick reflected smile from a baby's face, now a glance of apology or forgiveness for some fault, now a deep contentment in some shared pleasure—all will trace the endless variations of a tenderness no longer fiery but certainly real.

Married love is also *thoughtful*. The love which binds a man and woman together for life is one which is constantly concerned about the little things. If two people are going to live in close intimacy for a lifetime, knowing each other's inmost secrets of mind and body, they must be constantly aware of the little things that make the difference. To avoid that sensitive spot in a beloved's personality, to recall the little strengths with a compliment, to remember a birthday, an anniversary, a favorite song, a special taste, a preferred color-combination, is the kind of thoughtfulness that should characterize a husband and wife.

More important than the thoughtfulness for details is what might be called *implicit thoughtfulness*. It is easy for young lovers to recall the thoughtful little things necessary for a successful engagement. It might also be easy to do the same during the early days of marriage. But it is more important that the young lovers learn that everything they do in marriage, and for their marriage, must be with implicit thoughtfulness for their partner. A man who works hard to better himself at his work; who takes a scolding from his boss when, in his adolescent years, he might have quit in a huff; who hurries home in order to take an active interest in his wife and family; who worries about the mortgage and checks carefully the household budget; who exerts a leadership in his home in the education of his children; who concerns himself with the spiritual as well as with the temporal welfare of his wife and children—this man is always thoughtful of his beloved. He might not even give her a concrete thought all day long and yet, always on the edge of his consciousness, always guiding his actions, is his thoughtful married love.

In the same way a woman may not, after the first rapture of the honeymoon is over, think constantly of her young husband. She will seem to be lost in the duties of every day, cleaning her house, decorating it tastefully, cooking and serving attractive dinners, enduring the discomforts of pregnancy, changing the baby, separating hair-pulling daughters and quieting drum-thumping sons. She will now be concerned with thrifty shopping, with patiently educating and encouraging her children, inspiring the whole family with love and spiritual values. Yet all this can be done with implicit thoughtfulness for her partner. This kind of thoughtfulness is more important than remembering "the little things." Indeed, it is only from this kind of devotion that thoughtfulness in details flows.

When a man and a woman discover that their love is tender, and when they understand that this tenderness will change and vary through the years, and when, finally, they are willing to *let it vary*, they can hope that they have the start of true nuptial love. Yet, since the tenderness of young love during the engagement period can be so illusory, the more important sign is the mutual thoughtfulness, not only thoughtfulness that makes them concerned for the important little details, but also the implicit motivation which governs every one of their daily actions and directs those actions to each other.

LOVE IS CREATIVE

Wedded love is, by nature, creative. Intense devotion to a husband or wife quickly matures the young partner. Ask any young couple; they will tell you that, looking back upon their first day of marriage, they cannot believe that they were ever so young and so immature. Love encourages them to extend their creativity to their own personalities. A fun-loving adolescent girl who seemed intent only on the enjoyment of life, soon develops, under the impact of love, into a responsible young woman who finds her pleasure in keeping house, sharing the triumphs of her husband, accepting with joy the first difficulties of early pregnancy. Only love could have created this mature woman out of an immature adolescent. On the other hand, many a crew-cut young boy who roistered about the town with "the gang," now assumes the responsibilities of a young husband and father, pursuing advancement in his work and budgeting his small income cautiously. He is surprised at what he possesses when he discovers nuptial love.

True married love is the discovery of a second self in a partner. Whereas, before marriage, a person could devote all of his attention to his own self-development, now married love urges that the same amount of intensity be devoted to the development of the partner. Married love, then, becomes creative in the formation, unfolding, and development of the partner's potentialities. In deep love, this does not involve mutual nagging or needling; it involves constant mutual encouragement for each to achieve his full potentiality. Love rejoices in the successes of the beloved, and more, takes pride in each of those successes as though it were its own.

The third creativity of married love is children. Though many moderns talk excessively about the responsibility and burden which child-care and education place upon the parents, married love cannot help wanting a whole family of children. Just as the artist is never content with the canvas he has just finished—and which has come from his love-experience of the beautiful—so married lovers can never be content (all else being equal) with one child. One child contains and reflects some of the excellences of both partners but, alas, many of the defects of both. Though a husband may delight to see his wife's blue eyes in his son and a wife may be very happy to see the sturdy body so like his father's, creative love will yearn for ever-new combinations of the qualities which first led these two to fall in love with each other.

A painter who arbitrarily refused to paint after experiencing the beautiful—or one who paced himself at a certain number of canvasses a year—would soon discover that his aesthetic experiences became fewer and fewer, and farther and farther apart. Again, a young priest who might set an arbitrary limit on the number of confessions he intended to hear, or children he would baptize, or sermons he would preach, could hardly be said to be fully in love with God and God's children above all things.

All true love tends to creativity. Married love tends to overflow into progeny. In many cases, however, it happens that, though a loving husband and wife have developed their own personalities to the full, God does not send them any children. This is a sad blow to love. In many marriages, when this has happened, husband and wife have drifted far from each other, they have turned their creative impulses into materialistic pursuits. The doors of their garage could easily be marked "his" and "hers." Often enough, they drift so far apart that they resemble two people working in a strange city but merely keeping house together.

Married love must be creative in children in one fashion or another. It could easily become creative through adopting children. After all, mothering and fathering is not only a function of begetting; it is also one of educating, and many a couple have found creative satisfaction for their love in raising adopted children. Other young couples may find this creativity in the heart-warming—and yet heart-breaking—service of devoting themselves to foster children. They nurture these love-starved babies back to security and health for others. Perhaps they never see them grow to maturity, but their work is, nevertheless, creative love.

Finally, there are other couples who, facing the will of God that they will have no children of their own, dedicate themselves to the service of the community, and particularly to the needs of other families. Having more time to devote to public pursuits, they can, more easily than those who have a family, enter into political and social life to defend the rights of married love. The writer knows a school teacher and his wife (a registered nurse) who have never had a child of their own. Yet they can point with pride to literally thousands of young people born into other families whom they, themselves, have helped travel the path of growth to full maturity. Their home is a second home to every generation of teenagers in the town's high school. They have listened to and advised most of the young people when these youngsters have needed a second mother or father.

Married love, then, must be creative in its impact. It must unfold the personalities of the lovers; it must encourage and support the full development of the beloved; it must flower in children, whether natural or adoptive. Married love is God's way of sharing His own creativity with a man and woman.

Chapter Seven

GETTING MARRIED

GETTING READY

There is a story told of a baptismal party on a wintry Sunday evening. It seems that the relatives and friends of the parents who had just had their baby baptized came in to have an old-fashioned party. They hurried in, threw off their winter wraps on the bed, and entered the living room to warm themselves at the fireside and greet members of the family they had not seen since the last wake. After hours of chatting, eating, and drinking, and a song fest, someone remarked that he had not yet seen the baby. When the good parents looked for the child they could not find it. After an anxious search, the baby was pulled, screaming, from under the heap of winter clothing where it had almost smothered to death. The family had been so concerned with the party that they had forgotten the guest of honor!

Many young couples, in preparing for marriage, can draw a lesson from this story. Too many become so involved in the external preparations for marriage that they forget all about the sacrament of marriage itself. Some even forget that *they*, and not the wedding guests, are the most important. Immediately after the engagement ring has been given, most young couples enter into a flurry of excited preparations. They spend days being fitted in the best of finery, shopping for furniture, kitchenware, and an apartment. They spend agonizing hours in selecting the precise words for their wedding invitation, choosing the menu for their reception, and worrying whether they can safely seat Aunt Lydia near Uncle Tim who so cordially dislikes her. Frequently, this scurry of preparation leads to nervous tension, mutual irritability, and total oblivion to all spiritual preparation.

No matter how much you think you know about marriage and family life, the time of engagement should include more intense preparation for matrimony. Attend your local pre-Cana Conference or a series of lectures on preparation for marriage. Even though you have had a complete course in marriage preparation in high school or college, you will want to freshen up your knowledge and also have an opportunity to check your ideals and attitudes before your great day. There is a great advantage, as your wedding day comes closer, in listening to priests and married couples present marriage with the greatest of inner conviction. St. Paul says that "Faith . . . depends on hearing, and hearing on the word of Christ" (Rom. 10 : 17). A convinced speaker can transform your entire life and make something you have known all your life a reality which will be grasped not only by your mind but by your heart.

If you live in an area where marriage preparation series are few and far between, you can obtain much helpful information by correspondence. (Write for the correspondence version of *Together in Christ*, an eleven-lesson course available from the Family Life Bureau, National Catholic Welfare Conference, Washington 5, D.C.)

The time of engagement should also be a time of intense prayer and frequent reception of the sacraments. An engaged couple should not feel embarrassed to begin and end each date with a simple little prayer for their happiness and success in marriage. After all, in a brief time, they will be kneeling together each night to say their night prayers! This should not be a strange experience. It is very heartening to see so many engaged couples in the United States going to Mass and Communion together and reading the responses to the Dialogue Mass out of one missal. Such spiritual unity is a good indication that they will continue to strive together for the sanctity of their state of matrimony.

Gradually increasing in popularity are weekend retreats for engaged couples or engaged men or engaged women. If aspirants for religious life conclude their novitiate with a closed retreat before vowing themselves to God, how natural it should seem for the engaged to close their engagement "novitiate" with a retreat before pronouncing their vows to each other in God. If there is no retreat house in your area which offers you this opportunity, at least spend a weekly Holy Hour together for the few weeks before your marriage. Make sure that the last-minute preparations on the evening and morning before your wedding are not so full of scurry that you do not have time to pause for a moment in the presence of God to take stock in prayerful awareness of the great religious step you are taking.

Spiritual writers suggest that a general confession should always precede any change in one's state in life. This is a wise suggestion which should be followed a few days before your marriage. A general confession is absolutely necessary if you have deliberately concealed a serious sin in the past, if you have received any sacraments sacrilegiously and have never confessed it, or if any of your past confessions were invalid due to the absence of real sorrow or purpose of amendment. You are going to receive a sacrament of the living which demands that you be in the state of grace.

If, fortunately, there is no problem regarding past "bad" confessions, it is nevertheless a good idea to make a general review of your entire life so that you need never look back beyond the day of your entrance into this new calling in life.

A general confession is not difficult, nor should you fear it. Simply spend some time (usually with a printed exami-

nation of conscience) examining your life for all its faults
over the years. When you have a rather clear picture of
your life, enter the confessional and tell the confessor that
you wish to make a general confession because you are
soon to be married. Then ask him to help you by asking
questions. Within a very few minutes he will be able to
bring out all the serious sins of your past life and send
you forth with a joyous conviction that you are starting
your life together with an absolutely clean slate.

A wise novice master once told a group of young nov-
ices that on their profession day they would enter into
religious life as innocent as babies immediately after their
Baptism. There is no reason why the young Catholic couple should not start off their vocation to Christian matrimony with the same conviction.

THE ENGAGEMENT RING

Rings are symbols and not merely ornaments. A whole
history of the customs of mankind could be based upon
the different kinds of rings worn down through the ages.
Today, little children wear rings which are symbols and
tokens of their parents' love and affection. Many people
wear rings which contain their birthstones, to symbolize
their own importance as human beings. Men once wore
signet rings which were specially designed with their
family crest or initials so that they could be impressed
into the sealing wax that was used on public documents.
The rings were symbols of the integrity and dependability
of their owners. Most secondary school and college grad-
uates wear a special class ring which symbolizes their
loyalty to their alma maters and indicates the intellectual
achievement of their wearers. Bishops wear large rings
to indicate their authority over their flocks, their dedication in pure service to God, and their real "marriage" to
the diocese over which they are given charge.

The engagement ring is very meaningful for the young

couple. It is cast in a circle to signify the unbroken love to be exercised and developed by the couple. It also is a reminder that these two are *now* bound to each other in promise. An engagement ring is made of gold or some other precious metal which symbolizes the nobility and durability which should characterize the love exercised by these two. In modern times the engagement ring is crested with a diamond which flashes out both the purity and the fire of the love which has been pledged. If you have wondered why the engagement ring is worn upon the fourth finger of the left hand, it is interesting to notice that, in the early days of medicine, it was believed that the vein which led directly to the heart went through this finger.

All through the United States, young Catholic couples are becoming more and more aware of the sacredness of the marriage contract. As a result, they are beginning to demand even more symbolism in their engagement rings than was recognized up till now. Enthusiastic Catholic couples are beginning to exhibit engagement and wedding rings of more simple and less showy design which nevertheless have a deeper spiritual meaning. Some are of silver, enameled with liturgical symbols such as the chi-rho, the alpha and omega, the cross and crown, the vine and the branches, or a sheaf of wheat signifying the fruitfulness of love. Others are engraved with mottoes. For example, "Promised in Christ," "Thy Will be done," "United in Christ." Still others are engraved with phrases from Sacred Scripture, whether from the Old or New Testament.

Of course, liturgical engagement and wedding rings can become merely arty or showy jewelry which are selected just because they are "nice" or "different." But if an engagement ring is selected because of the real meaning it has for the engaged couple, it not only can mean a great deal in their hearts but also can actually bring about a transformation and deepening of their spiritual lives. Since a human being is composed of both body and soul, not only does he arrange the outside world symbolically, because of his inner spirit, but his inner spirit is also affected by the outside world. It should be a thrilling and meaningful experience for the young couple to design or select an engagement ring which expresses fully, in symbolic fashion, their love for each other in Christ.

SANCTIFYING THE ENGAGEMENT

If marriage and family life is a way of knowing, loving, and serving God; if marriage is a real vocation from God to serve Him in a special way, then the period of engagement should be a period of intense spiritual preparation for the reception of the sacrament of Matrimony and for the holy life which must follow. Isn't it strange, then, that most engagements begin when the young man slips an engagement ring on the left ring-finger of his future bride in a darkened car or living room? Her squeal of (feigned?) surprise, her enthusiastic kiss, seem more like signs of triumph that she has "nailed down" her man than of her reverent joy that a life of dedicated service to God will soon begin.

Engagements were not so casual in past ages. Primitive tribes, the early Greeks and Romans, all major nationality groups, prescribed elaborate rituals for the contract to marry which is an engagement. True, many of these rituals seemed solely concerned with the barter price for the bride, the extent of the dowry, the advantages to the two families, and other financial considerations; but all of them implied deep awareness of the seriousness of such a contract and the religious nature of the state contracted for.

The Catholic Church has, throughout its history, been deeply concerned with the spiritual nature and meaning of engagements. In the third century Tertullian mentioned the spiritual signification of engagement ceremonies. The scholarly St. Augustine mentions that the bishop himself should sign the Christian engagement contract. St. Thomas points out a kind of sacramental meaning for the engagement ceremony. Ecclesiastical law has always had regulations concerning the nature, validity, extent, and spirituality of the contract to marry. Since the custom of formal, legal, or solemn engagement has faded in many areas, most American Catholics are not aware that, even in the present Code of Canon Law, there are special prescriptions for the solemn engagement (Canon 1017).

The solemn engagement, as described in Church law, is a legal instrument which either or both parties sign, contracting to marry the other within a certain time. This legal document is witnessed either by the bishop or the pastor or before two witnesses. Though the agreement will not force a couple to enter into a possibly unwilling marriage, there must be seriously justifying reasons in order to break such an engagement. If one party unjustly breaks the engagement, he is bound in conscience to restore to the other all expenses incurred in view of the preparation for marriage. He may even be sued in a Church court for the recovery of such expenses if he refuses to make good. The signed contract to marry is recorded and filed in the archives of the church.

Church law merely indicates the *legal* requirements for the solemn engagement, but it also implies the customary beautiful religious ceremony as a sanctifying element for the contract.

Many of our young people, in rebellion against the secular and frivolous engagements so often entered into within our country, are beginning to demand a truly religious engagement so that they can spiritualize their novitiate for marriage. They are beginning to insist that their engagement, as every other important event of their lives, begin in church.

There is no official liturgical ceremony for the solemn

engagement. However, there are several approved ones which may be used. Usually the young couple, with their witnesses, quietly enter the church and go up to the communion rail. The priest, vested in surplice and white stole, and with holy water and an altar missal, stands before them. The beautiful psalm, "Unless the house be of the Lord's building, in vain do the builders labor" (Psalm 126), is either sung or recited. The priest then gives them a brief address, pointing out the joys of the holy vocation of matrimony, their prayerful consideration of each other as future spouses, the need for seeking good advice in their choice, the need to prepare for the sacrament of Matrimony by a period of chaste courtship, and the beautiful longing they have to consummate their union as man and wife as a sacramental image of the union of Christ and His Bride, the Church.

The couple joins their right hands and the future husband gives his promise to marry: "In the name of Our Lord, I, John Smith, promise that I will one day take thee, Susan Brown, as my wife according to the ordinances of God and Holy Church. I will love thee even as myself; I will keep faith and loyalty to thee, and so, in thy necessities, aid and comfort thee; which things and all that a man ought to do unto his espoused I promise to do unto thee and to keep by the faith that is in me."

The future bride repeats the same promise and the priest then places his stole in the form of a cross over the clasped hands of the couple while he bears witness of their solemn proposal to marry. He then sprinkles them with holy water and blesses the engagement ring, which the future groom places on the index finger of the left hand of his bride-to-be, saying, "In the name of the Father"; then, on the middle finger, adding, "And of the Son"; and finally leaving it on the ring finger, concluding, "And of the Holy Spirit." After both kiss the altar missal, the Old Testament description of the betrothal and wedding of Tobias and Sara is read, or else some passages from the Gospel of St. John.

This is a thrilling and meaningful ceremony. Don't let your engagement be merely a secular event whose success is measured by the size of your diamond or the envy of your friends. Your engagement is the immediate preparation for the vocation of marriage and family life; your engagement should be in church.

RED TAPE?

Americans, though they are generally law-abiding people, have a very peculiar attitude towards the laws which govern them. Jealous of their own individual freedom, and frequent in their use of such phrases as "It's a private affair," "It's nobody else's business," Americans approach the law with a very suspicious attitude. Many young couples approaching their marriage have a similar attitude towards meeting the priest. They expect to go to him merely to arrange the date and time of their wedding and frequently feel resentful if he starts asking them questions. Lost as they are in their own love for each other, they will brook no interference, no advice, no suggestions, and hence they tend to resent the regulations which both civil and ecclesiastical law impose upon them before they can effectively marry.

Americans feel that law is a hurdle or wall which keeps them from doing what they have every right to do. They almost imagine God and other law-givers saying, "People seem to be enjoying themselves; let's see what we can do to stop it." No, law is not meant to stop activity but to direct it towards its goal. The levees on the Mississippi River, though they restrain the river, do not prevent it from draining the countryside, but attempt to insure that it will perform its function. In the same way, law is a reasonable command which attempts to direct proper activity to its intended goal. It also protects others and the common good, as well as the individual good. The required instructions on your medicine bottle indicate how this medicine can be used to bring about health. The "poison" symbol on that same bottle may point out that others may be harmed if they do not use this medicine according to instructions. So it is with the religious and civil laws which govern marriage. These laws are not so much "red tape" to irk lovers and keep them apart; these laws are designed to make sure that the lovers are fully, freely, and permanently in love. Other laws are necessary to protect society, which has such a deep stake in the success or failure of their union. Law is there to help make married love *sure*.

Several months before the date upon which you would like to be married you should call the parish priest on the phone to make an appointment with him to set your date. He might wish to see you immediately or he might settle the simple matter of date and time over the telephone. Then he will make an appointment with you to come in about six weeks before your marriage and go through the "pre-nuptial investigation." There is no need to become irritated or anxious about this investigation. It is required by Church law to make sure that you are free to marry, that you are old enough to make up your own mind, that there are no impediments to your union, and that, in general, nothing else is present which could, in any way, interfere with the complete validity and lawfulness of your union.

In recent years most dioceses have set up a form to be used for this investigation. This form varies from diocese to diocese, but always includes a list of questions that are proposed, individually, to the prospective bride and groom. The priest wants to know who you are, so he asks the usual points of identification: name, address, birth, names of parents, age and religious background. Secondly, he wishes to know whether there are any impediments which would render your marriage either unlawful or void. Therefore, he questions you about the various degrees of relationship and other impediments you learned so clearly in your days in catechism class. Thirdly, he wants to know whether you honestly and freely wish to enter marriage with this particular person and whether you know what married life is. In other words, he wishes to know whether you understand "what you are getting into." Therefore, he asks a number of questions about your understanding of marriage and its obligations, and whether you have been subjected to any kind of pressure to marry this person.

The questions are presented to you under oath to remind you how important they are and how solemnly you must consider your answers. They are also asked you while you are apart from your partner. Many young people wonder what is going on while they are sitting outside paging through the back-issues of magazines. Only one question will be asked of your partner about yourself. This question concerns your honest willingness to enter the marriage.

Once the form is filled out, it is witnessed by the priest and the signed form is preserved in the files of the parish. All this helps to make your marriage a permanent one. Should you wish to call at the rectory some five years from now and say that you didn't mean to get married, you will have a difficult time proving that the answers you gave under oath and before a witness were false.

There are many documents required for marriage. The priest will need a recently filled out baptismal certificate and, since he expects his people to marry only after they are mature, he also will demand a certificate of Confirmation. (Confirmation, of course, is the sacrament of spiritual adulthood.) If you have not, as yet, been confirmed, it is still possible to marry validly, but the Church prefers you to have been confirmed first.

The civil community also has many requirements. It

will require medical certificates and a "Declaration of Intention to Marry" or marriage license. Naturally, the priest will want to make sure that all these are in order.

Please give the priest plenty of time for his "paper work." Many young people have been moving from one city or state to another for most of their lifetime. It is necessary for the priest who performs your wedding to send inquiries to every place that you have lived for six months or more since your fourteenth birthday to make sure that there is no record of your having contracted a marriage during that time. These inquiries are not a questioning of your good faith and veracity; they are simply a determination that no question can ever be raised about the validity of your union in the future.

Finally, the priest must have enough time to announce the banns of marriage. These are formal public proclamations that must be made on three successive Sundays or Holydays of Obligation at the parish Mass in the churches of both bride and groom and in every parish in which they have lived for a notable time since they have been fourteen years of age. The purpose of the banns is to discover whether the members of the parish know of any real reason why the couple should not be permitted to marry. This again is a protection of the couple and of the community. Your love, which you intend to consummate in Christian marriage, a miniature Mystical Body, is of intense concern to the entire Mystical Body of Christ and to the civic community within which you live. By all means, go to hear your banns proclaimed. You should be proud to hear your love published to the community.

MARRY AT MASS!

I can never understand the desire of some young couples to have a "fashionable" afternoon wedding without the Nuptial Mass. I know that these marriages are just as valid and sacramental as those performed at Mass but, somehow, they always leave me somewhat saddened. The wedding party comes into the church to the solemn peal of the wedding march; the partners say their vows, slip on the wedding rings, are sprinkled with holy water, and then turn to go out again. It is all over in a few minutes.

If at all possible, the Catholic couple should be united in Christian matrimony at a Nuptial Mass. At a Nuptial Mass, the bride and groom enter into the holy of holies, the sanctuary, for the only occasion of their lifetimes. They give and receive their nuptial vows, they perform the sacrament of Matrimony for each other in the presence of a priest richly garbed in the full vestments of his office. They participate in a Mass which is specially written for them and their needs. Every word of the Mass proper refers to the spiritual riches of their state. At the Pater Noster the priest interrupts the Canon of the Mass to invite the young couple to kneel on the upper altar step while he reads over them, in the presence of their sacramental Lord, the special nuptial blessing which can be given at no other time without a special dispensation of the bishop. At the Communion, the bride and groom become one with Christ and, in becoming one with Him, they are closer to each other than at any other moment in their marital lives, even in the most apparently intimate ones.

If you, as bride and groom, are going to symbolize and relive the union of Christ and His Church in your sacrament of Matrimony, why not start off that union at Mass when Christ, the Divine bridegroom, comes to meet His bride, the Church?

This is your day, as important for you as the ordination day of a priest. If possible, then, why not the most solemn Mass possible? Why not a Solemn High Mass or at least a Missa Cantata (sung Mass)? If neither seems possible, let me urge the Dialogue Mass, when the Church, in the person of all your relatives and friends, can join with you in offering your Mass to God through the priest. Do not feel embarrassed if you have invited many non-Catholic friends. Let them follow the Nuptial Mass in a booklet so that they can understand the religious life which you live and its impact upon Christian family living.

If your pastor approves, by all means invite all your Catholic friends and relatives to receive Holy Communion with you and for you on your great day. With the modern laws on fasting before Holy Communion, it should be very easy for them to join with you in Holy Communion no matter how late in the morning the hour of your Nuptial Mass. Since you are starting a new cell in Christ's Mystical Body, how wonderful to know that your friends within the Body of Christ are seconding your vocational choice by their active participation in the Mass and the reception of Holy Communion.

THE WEDDING FEAST

What does "wedding feast" bring to mind? Laughter, a reception line, toasts to the bride, good food and drink, music, the bride's waltz, dancing, pictures, hurrying off for the wedding trip under the cheers and shouted good wishes of your friends? It should be all these things and more. Sometimes Catholics are accused of being opposed to "good times." When we talk of Christianizing our modern world, people sometimes think we mean the killing off of human joys. Certainly not! Remember that Christ performed His first miracle at a wedding feast. His miracle, so far as we can understand, was not performed to win converts or to cure the sick. It was performed as a practical measure, a neighborly gesture, to help the wedding feast to be even more joyous with a sufficient amount of wine!

Without losing any of the natural joy and gaiety, without forgetting a single little item of natural satisfaction, please do not forget to make of your wedding feast a really Christian affair. Center your wedding invitations, the decorations on your wedding cake, your place-cards and napkins upon liturgical and religious symbols of marriage. Invite the priest who celebrated your Nuptial Mass to your wedding breakfast or reception. No matter how busy he is, he can at least stop by to bless the wine for your toast. You will see in him the presence of Christ at your own Cana.

A new custom is growing: that of the young couple purchasing a little silver bell to be used at their Nuptial Mass. This bell is placed at the bridal table and is used to get the attention of your guests for your toasts, prayer before meals, and your little speeches. It then will find a place among your memories and in your home and will recall the first hour of your family life which actually began in the sanctuary.

In some parishes, the bride may make a simple corporal which is used by the celebrant of the Nuptial Mass. After Mass, the priest rinses it and returns it to the couple. Later it will be used in the home during sick calls—another way of reminding you that your home will be a "Church in miniature."

Why not make your "bride's waltz" a dedication to our Lady, spouse of the Holy Spirit and spouse to St. Joseph? We have forgotten the meaning of the religious dance. In Spain, solemn dances are performed within the church on all notable occasions!

As you pack and leave for your wedding trip, make sure that you include not only the old custom of "something new and something old" but also the cherished religious symbols of your lifetime. Many priests give the young couple a crucifix as they congratulate them at the foot of the altar. Take it or your cherished picture or statue along on your wedding trip. There is as much joy in the cross as there is in your mutual love for which you will sacrifice everything else. Indeed, your Christian married love *is* the same love which drove Christ to ascend His Cross in order that His Bride, the Church, might be "without blemish."

THE HONEYMOON

Many young couples wonder about the wisdom of going on a honeymoon. On the one hand, they know they would enjoy a beautiful, idyllic trip together. Often they realize this may be their last opportunity for such a trip, since the financial responsibilities of home and family will soon be upon them. On the other hand, staid old-timers might tell them that "someday you will wish you had that honeymoon money back." Some advisors suggest that the honeymoon is one of the most delightful ways of beginning to know each other intimately and of starting out in the best possible manner. Others feel that the honeymoon so romanticizes and embroiders reality that, far from being a help, it is a hindrance.

Someday someone will write a history of the honeymoon custom. Why do we have the honeymoon anyway? I think it is because people have discovered through the centuries that no matter how well they knew each other during courtship, the proximity of intimate life, day after day, can be revealing to the point of shock! After all, courtship was a time to win your partner. So you put your best foot forward. You don't let him know anything about those odd little personal quirks which you have tried to correct all your life. Since you took each other "for better or worse" you must now begin to learn those little oddities with which you will live for the rest of your life.

Young couples have also felt the need of privacy in which to make their first adjustments, particularly in the area of bodily love. It seemed wise to go off somewhere together in the most relaxed atmosphere rather than to attempt the discovery of each other during the business of earning a living or at the beck and call of well-meaning friends. Psychologists generally agree with this.

Cost. When you choose your honeymoon site, certainly you should consider the cost. A fabulous hotel will be scant consolation if it takes you several years of your married life to pay off the bill. On the other hand, sensible mutual generosity will shrink from niggardliness. Mutual generosity, which does not put you head-over-heels into debt, should not make you feel guilty, nor draw you to look back at your several hundred dollars expense with regret. If you have initiated a good marital adjustment on your honeymoon the money was well spent.

Choice. Some young couples decide to take an extended tour and they tend to measure the success of their trip in terms of the number of miles they have covered, the number of places they have seen, the number of steps they have taken. They are very foolish. Utter weariness is no condition in which to initiate the intimate togetherness of marriage. If you choose to tour, set no goals of achievement, make your hours together hours of relaxation and not of boredom. Though reasonable recreation in some vacation spot may be quite enjoyable, make sure that you do not spend all of your time with other members of a group, even though they themselves are honeymooners. Group activities may get you out of yourselves, but this is not your goal. You are beginning a life of mutual involvement.

Enthusiasm. Be enthusiastic about your honeymoon. Some people are afraid to enjoy themselves for fear that they will come down to reality with a great thump. Of course, if you are so unrealistic as to believe that "my honeymoon will last forever" you are in for a rude awakening. Though the cake is more than the icing, the meal more than the dessert, the marriage more than the honeymoon, don't hesitate to enjoy the icing, the dessert, the romance.

The only important thing in the honeymoon is to secure enough privacy and enough opportunity to really explore each other's personalities. This can be achieved in romantic and luxurious surroundings, or it can be achieved in a cottage in the woods, an off-season vacation spot, or even in your own little apartment, so long as nobody knows you are home.

Do honeymooners adore each other? Probably, but they had better beware lest they leave God out of the picture. God *is* love and to attempt to leave him out is to expel love from love! Sunday Mass should go into your honeymoon schedule as well as daily prayer together. A good start involves your start towards God and heaven as a team.

Chapter Eight

CHILDREN?

READ THE INSTRUCTIONS

The first thing you do when you buy a new machine, whether it is an automatic washer or a power drill, is to read the manufacturer's instructions. If you want to use the machine wisely, you must know precisely why it was made, what it can do, and how to use it. You will make many mistakes and perhaps destroy what it cost you a great sacrifice to purchase, if you do not carefully read the manufacturer's instructions first. Doesn't it make sense then, to ask yourself what the "manufacturer" has prescribed about marriage, instead of rushing headlong into it without knowing why it was made, what it can do, and how to use it?

What does God think of marriage? What is it for, in His plan? How do you effectively use marriage according to the God who invented it? Let's take a look at Sacred Scripture to find out. In reading Scripture, however, we must remember that God is made to look "human" there so that our weak minds can catch a reflection of His power. There is no time or deliberation, no moving from action to action, no process of reasoning in God. But Scriptural writers "humanize" God so we can catch a simplified idea of His wisdom and how He carries it out.

God created the world in six days—six periods of time. During the first five of these "days" He created all the glories of the universe—the sun, the moon, the stars, the beauties of the foliage, everything from the magnificent

133

galaxies of stars in the firmament to the myriad treasures in the depths of the sea. Yet, each one of these things He created by a simple act of His will. He simply said, "Let there be light," and light was made. Each act of creation seems to have come immediately, without deliberation, from the mind of God. After each creation God looked at the result and "saw that it was good."

The creation of man was quite different. When, on the sixth day, the time came to create man, God is pictured as deliberating within Himself, as entering into a sort of discussion within the Trinity, as though this creation should be more deliberate, more careful. After taking counsel, He concluded "Let us make mankind in our own image and likeness" (Gen. 1: 26). The decision made, He did not simply command, "Let there be man." He went through an ordered process. Scripture tells us that God formed the body of man from the slime of the earth, and then He breathed into this man His own spirit.

God put this man, whom He had made to His own image and likeness, in His garden of paradise. He paraded before Adam all of the animals in the garden and asked Adam to name each one. Now, in the Old Testament, naming things is a very important privilege. The right to give a name indicated that the person possessing the right also had power over the object named. But after reviewing all these wondrous creations placed under his command, Adam was not yet content. We read one of the saddest lines in all Scripture when we read, "he [Adam] found no helper like himself" (Gen. 2: 20).

God is again pictured as retiring into Himself to discuss this matter of the loneliness of Adam. God is not resting in the goodness of His creation this time! He concludes, "It is not good that the man is alone; I will make him a helper like himself" (Gen. 2: 18). So God cast a deep sleep upon Adam, took a rib from his side, formed from that rib another human body, breathed a soul into it, and then awakened Adam.

God, the first matchmaker, now led this new creation, the woman, to Adam. When Adam saw her, he broke into the first poetic utterance in the Old Testament—a love poem. "She now is bone of my bone, and flesh of my flesh; she shall be called Woman, for from man she has been taken" (Gen. 2: 23).

After uniting Adam and Eve in marriage, God gave them a blessing. A blessing means a wish for happiness. This was God's blessing: "Be fruitful and multiply; fill the earth" (Gen. 1:28). In other words Adam and Eve were to find their happiness in being fruitful and in filling the earth with children. Scripture continues, "The man knew Eve his wife, and she conceived and bore Cain, saying: 'I have given birth to a man-child with the help of the Lord' " (Gen. 4:1). Here was an exclamation of joy— the joy that comes from marriage as God wishes it to be lived.

Besides the instructions on the tools you buy, there may well be other recommendations. The manufacturer may suggest the kind of lubrication to use. He may urge you to have the tool demonstrated, so that you fully understand it. He may have examples of its use pictured, and of what to do if it fails. He may even suggest places where it can be repaired.

Throughout Scripture we find many suggestions, examples, and models of what marriage is all about. The story of Tobias and Sara, for example, shows how a young couple should not give themselves to their lust. The unhappy adultery of David, the temptation of Susanna, give examples of how *not* to use marriage. But let us skip quickly to the instructions of Christ, who says, "Have you not read that the Creator, from the beginning, made them male and female, and said, 'For this cause a man shall leave his father and mother, and cleave to his wife, and the two shall become one flesh'? Therefore now they are no longer two, but one flesh. What therefore God has joined together, let no man put asunder" (Matt. 19:5-7). Our Lord is here concerned that the unity of marriage shall never be broken or even weakened.

As we ponder over these prescriptions for the happiness of marriage, we notice that God seems first concerned with the loneliness of Adam—and certainly the young couple can well start into marriage full of the love which dispels the tremendous sense of loneliness that each of us has in the face of a unique destiny. Though this reason was first, chronologically, it was not primary in importance. Adam and Eve were ordained to find their happiness, their blessing, in *children*. In the staid legal language of the Code of Canon Law, the Church declares that marriage has as its objective "the procreation and education of children"—a cold definition, but one in which the prescription for success and happiness in marriage lies.

Once the young married couple truly seek their happiness in family life, then they can discover the joys of romance, the delightful division of labor which fills out each other's needs, the true deep satisfaction of sexual experience together, and the happiness which flows from mutual enjoyment of pleasures and material things. But all this depends upon their choosing for themselves what God Himself has chosen for them—family life. Our Lord says, "But seek the kingdom of God, and all these things shall be given you besides" (Luke 12: 31). The kingdom of God for you in marriage is family living with all its chores and duties. Our Lord tells us in effect: "If you seek all these other joys, you will obtain nothing. But if you put in the proper place over all your hoping and planning and working, the duties of marriage and family life, all the other joys you can dream of will come to you besides."

SHALL WE HAVE CHILDREN?

In years gone by this was a silly question. Every young couple who entered marriage took it for granted that a family would flow from their love just as summer follows the spring. Young people several generations ago knew nothing of the generative process, and therefore accepted the children as they came. Nevertheless, I do not believe that our great-grandparents were notably more religious than parents today; they simply accepted what they could not do anything about. In some ways it was a healthier kind of living, since it did not present them with the modern problems of choice.

Today, modern science enables the young husband and wife to know when they are liable to become parents and therefore presents them with a series of almost frightening choices. The young couple of today, knowing what they know about conception and pregnancy, though they can be selfish, can also be more freely and fully at the service of God's providence by making wise choices.

Yet it seems strange that a man and a woman entering marriage should even ask themselves this question. Some modern marriage counselors suggest that the young couple should postpone their first child for a year or two in order to become better acquainted. Though I can conceive of such advice being given to a specific couple, I suspect that the true advice should have been a suggestion that they remain unmarried a year or two longer until they are ready for real married love. Why must we keep people perpetually adolescent?

When a young couple enter marriage with the enthusiasm of young love, it should be the natural thing to anticipate a family. Each will desire that the qualities they admired in the other shall be combined in ever new combinations as their young family grows. If human generation were perfect, it would combine the perfections of both father and mother, and mirror the faults of neither. In the Trinity, whose life the married couple mirrors, there is only one Son, who is the perfectly uttered Word of the Father. But human generation is not perfect. Just as the artist's love for the beautiful is not content with one canvas for each vision, so the love of husband and wife is not naturally content with one or two imperfect reflections of their enthusiasm.

When and if the time comes that social pressure, financial difficulties, physical illness, or eugenic fears indicate the prudence of limiting a family, the young couple will reluctantly choose the moral means of permanent or periodic continence, and pray for the day when Christian prudence will suggest that they continue their family growth.

Natural love urges the young couple to have children. Supernatural married love raises this natural enthusiasm to the plane of divine Love itself. Christian spouses are so in love with God, and each other in God, that they tend to desire little ones to share their divine love. Deeply aware that God Himself is involved in the begetting of each child, they want to raise divine lovers.

PARENTS SHOULD BE PROUD

One sometimes wonders why parents have children. In many cases is seems that the children just happen, and are accepted merely as the necessary evil resulting from the desire of two people for living together.

Judging from the way some parents treat their children, you might guess that they have a child just to show him off. They like to talk about the cute sayings that the youngster comes up with. They dress him prettily, like a doll to be placed in a collection cabinet. They insist that the child shall always be "a credit to them." They use the child to extend themselves into areas which they themselves were unable to enter: "My child is going to do all those things that I couldn't do."

Sometimes one suspects that the children are allowed to come into being simply for their usefulness. At least for a few years they can be made to be companions. They are useful for running errands; to act as trained little servants; and to support their parents in their old age.

This last is, of course, extremely problematical because it is the universal experience that just when a boy grows up enough to contribute something to the household, some girl comes along and *gets the interest.*

But why should a child be accepted when he comes into the world? A child should be accepted simply because he is a human being. Every human being has the right to be loved or accepted merely for the fact that he is, not for what he can do or what he can contribute. In our democracy we insist that a man has rights not because of his intelligence or his stature or his lineage, but simply because he is a human being. The very fact that he exists is sufficient. A child, therefore, should be received simply for himself. Home, at least, should be the place where a child is accepted not for what he can contribute or earn but simply for his existence.

But the human being does not exist simply for himself. He exists for God. St. Francis de Sales says that the purpose of parenthood is to people the earth with adorers of God and to fill heaven with saints. A child is, therefore, desirable out of love of God. The poet who falls in love wants everyone to read his poem about his beloved so that all may come to worship at her shrine. The priest who accepts his vocation will constantly and joyfully mount the pulpit or pick up his pen in order to convert all the world to love the God whom he loves. So also the apostolate of parents is to present to God fresh new adorers. If the commandment to love God above all things is valid, it means that parents in their parenthood must love God above all things, presenting their children to him.

Just think what this means: Each child you will bear is absolutely unique. There never was nor will there ever be another person precisely like him. Though he has a beginning at the moment of conception, he will never have an end. For all eternity he will continue to live either in the love and happiness of God or in the hatred and misery of hellfire. Further, he is called to share not merely the full intellectual and volitional happiness of knowing about God, but the very knowing and loving which God has for Himself. This divine life will be given to him when you present him at the baptismal font, but it will be for the child to develop that divine life to the fullness of his birth to heaven. With St. Paul your child is called to cry out "Abba" (Father!) to God. He can only do this in any full sense if he achieves a participation in the nature of God through grace, because a father is one who gives his own life to a child. This child, therefore, has the very inheritance of Jesus Christ Himself. St. Paul says: "But if we are sons, we are heirs also: heirs indeed of God and joint heirs with Christ, provided, however, we suffer with Him that we may also be glorified with Him" (Rom. 8:17).

Lastly your child by Baptism is incorporated into the Mystical Body of Christ. This means that he is really and truly a member of Christ's body, not in a physical but in a mystical, yet no less real, sense. Since Christ did not choose to perpetuate His human nature on earth down all the ages, the only way that He can reach the twentieth century is through His members—you and your children. His voice can only be heard through their voice. His feet can only walk in the twentieth century in their footsteps. His hands can bind up the wounds of the world only through their hands. To give Christ hands and feet and voice is part of the vocation of Christian parenthood.

How different the reason for Christian parents to have children than the reason which pagan parents use. The highest motives that pagan parents can have is to love their children for themselves. Christian parents not only love children for themselves but in and for God.

It follows then that this spiritual reason is the foundation for Christian parenthood; the large family is a Christian ideal granted that it is possible to accept this large number physically, economically, socially.

Must parents then avidly seek to have all the children they possibly can? Does this mean that the primary purpose of marriage—the procreation and education of children—should be their main reason for getting married? If so, then the proposal would sound something like, "I notice that the birth rate is falling, let's you and I get together and do something about it!" No, it is enough that, in the love of a bride and groom, there be the *implicit* desire for children. It is a matter of accepting God's will as to family size. It is not a case of having the number of children you'd love, but of loving the number you have.

If all this is true, there should be a measure of pride and self-respect in Christian parents. Many men are proud of their position in life, the income they obtain, their prowess on the golf course. Many women are happy in their beauty, their skill at bridge, their position in the League of Women Voters. How many parents are proud of parenthood?

Chapter Nine

SETTLING DOWN

DOWN TO EARTH

I wonder whether experienced married couples are not a bit jealous of the enthusiasm which they discover in a young married couple. Do they perhaps yearn to return to the days of their own early romance? Or are they trying to help a young couple be realistic when they say, "Well, the honeymoon's over now, it's time for you to settle down"?

The enthusiasm of young love is a wonderful invention of God. The searing intensity of this love, far from being a mistake or an accident, is given to the young couple so that they may build the quiet warmth and calm determination to promote each other's good which is the reality of love. It is only necessary that the young husband and wife realize that they cannot warm themselves for life merely by striking matches. It is not at all necessary for them to reject and suspect the enthusiasm of natural love. Each step of living, each step of growth, should be savored to the full, and yet not clasped to one's self as though it would last forever.

Sometimes when the first enthusiasms have begun to fade, a young couple will become panic-stricken and rush off to a "second honeymoon." Sometimes they even rush back to the place where they discovered their first enthusiastic adjustments, only to find that it is just another summer resort or primitive cottage in the woods. The place does not make the honeymoon, the couple does. It is not necessary to make life a perpetual honeymoon. In fact such a life would be emotionally exhausting, and any intense pleasure can become disgusting if it is constant.

The young religious goes through the same sort of enthusiastic honeymoon as does the young married couple. During the novitiate he enthusiastically chooses God. Nothing seems too difficult. He embraces prayer and mortification with an abandon that makes the more mature religious almost wince. But the enthusiasm of the young religious does not last forever. God takes away the candy of enthusiasm to see whether the young religious loves the candy more than the Giver; the gifts of God more than the God of gifts. So in marriage the thrills must fade by an inexorable law of nature, so that the young couple can discover whether they love merely the thrill of giving, or the beloved to whom the gift is given.

One wonders whether people really understand how life is lived. Some give the impression that they are only living when they are having fun. Their work, whether in the office, the factory, or the home, seems to them merely a hurdle to get over so they can enjoy themselves and live. As a matter of fact, it is the work which is the living and the pleasure which makes the work possible. Pleasure is the grease for the wheels. But the wheels transport the huge loads over the ground. Romance makes easier the work of keeping each partner happy, but it is the work of devotion to each other which builds the reality of a Christian marriage. Warmed by the emotional romance, the young couple must settle down to build the magnificent structure which is a good Christian family. There will be many successes and many failures, but as the years go on and smooth features turn to wrinkles, and beautiful physiques sag, the family that these two build, and the building process itself, will bring them more joy than all the thrills of early honeymoon romance. Yet the honeymoon is there to send them off to a flying start.

WORKING BRIDES

After the honeymoon, most young brides return to the jobs they held before marriage, and continue to bring home a pay check until the first baby is due. I wonder whether this is always wise. If you were to take a survey of mature married women who have started off their married lives by working for a pay check, I am sure that you would come up with a great variety of opinions. Many wives and mothers are happy that they worked during their earlier years, because they were able to pay off some of the debt of getting started. Others feel that remaining alone in a small apartment all day, and in some cases for days at a time, would have sent them out screaming for companionship. On the other hand, there are other things to be considered. One young mother said to me: "All that I ever learned about cooking or housekeeping I learned before the birth of my first child. I have never had time since then to learn anything really new." Another mother said: "I'm glad I stayed at home from the beginning. I got used to being alone during the day and when I had a rather difficult pregnancy I was able to live with myself. If I had been forced into a sudden transition from a busy office life to living alone with my 'complications' I would have gone out of my mind." Still another wife told me: "The double pay check was so nice to live on, that when we were forced to live on a single income we almost resented the baby!" Finally, one wife suggested: "Though I worked for about a year after our marriage and managed to pay off most of our furniture bills, the combination of a typewriter and vacuum cleaner, of filing and cooking kept me so tired and tense that many of our early arguments started from no other reason than that I was too tired to be reasonable."

I wonder whether we should not also poll the opinions of young husbands and fathers on the subject of allowing their brides to work. One young husband indicated: "I was most grateful that Claire was able to work at her secretarial job for a year after our marriage. It really got us off to a firm financial basis, but it was tough sledding for the both of us. We both had to pitch in to keep the apartment in order, do the cooking, dishes, and so on." Another husband reports: "I hate to come into an empty house. In our early marriage I frequently came home before my wife could get back from the city and sometimes we met entering the apartment together, and both had to face the unmade beds. Personally I'd rather do without the little extras we could have had and be met by a relaxed smiling wife with a real home-cooked meal." Still another asks: "What did we really save by the experience of Barbara working? After we paid our double taxes, checked off deductions, paid for her transportation, clothing and office collections—after we calculated the cost of frozen foods, or sneaking out guiltily to restaurants, we concluded that for all practical purposes we were losing money."

No young bride should feel guilty if she works after marriage, if her choice of work is fully approved by her husband and if the couple really agrees to work together in setting up house, and no notable tensions arise. On the other hand, the young bride should not be made to feel guilty because she prefers to stay at home and learn those household arts which will stand her in such good stead during the years she must stay home to raise her children.

Brides with vivacious, outgoing personalities may feel that a three-room apartment will not keep them busy enough and that they will feel almost imprisoned in such a small space. This is true if they concentrate merely on keeping house and making one full meal for the working husband. But there are many other household skills that can be learned very easily. Courses in sewing are provided by most sewing-machine manufacturers. Adult education courses on child care, nutrition, interior decorating, and home economics are available in most urban areas free of charge or for a nominal fee. The smart young home-maker will not pass up these opportunities. A few months of intensive study and practice will pay rich dividends in endlessly varied menus, delightful home color-schemes, beautifully though frugally dressed children, contented husbands, well disciplined children and real feminine pride and satisfaction in a well managed home.

Our conclusion? Consider all the reasons for and against working during the early years of marriage, and make up your own mind. If what you decide is by real agreement and for the good of your marriage, you will not be wrong.

SIGNS OF LOVE

How attentive the young engaged couple is towards each other! Their faces light up as they meet each other; they are constantly solicitous for each other's comfort; little gifts exchange hands; both try to outdo each other in mutual service.

It is extremely difficult to explain why these actions which mean so much to each other during courtship are so frequently forgotten as marriage progresses. This is not to say that the intense emotional services that were so thrilling during courtship should necessarily continue in marriage. No one could continue to live for a lifetime at that pitch.

What probably happens after marriage is that both partners settle down and become interested in their natural pursuits as wife and husband, mother and father. Then, almost unconsciously, they forget the little detailed actions towards each other that mean so much. They feel certain that the other partner must know that, whatever they are doing, they are doing it for him.

Once the young husband has won his bride, he tends to take it for granted that he has paid her the supreme compliment of her life in asking her to be his wife! Maturing rapidly from the rather adolescent youngster he was during courtship, he now devotes himself to building a home and income. Whereas before he used to remember the simple little gift, the carefully selected card for her birthday or anniversary, and the chivalrous and polite things to do, he now tends to omit these as marriage goes along. A barbed quip remarks that, when a man opens the car door for his wife and closes it carefully, you can be certain that either the car or the wife is new!

Just as a woman tends to look behind her husband's words to see whether there could possibly be any hidden meaning, so she tends to look behind his actions or omissions for hidden meanings. She suspects, if he no longer brings her the thoughtful gift, that he no longer loves her. If he forgets a wedding anniversary it proves he has forgotten *her*. As a matter of fact, however, though actions should continue to bespeak love, these omissions from the point of view of a man seldom mean anything other than that he is abstracted in his work or that he has simply forgotten in the pressure of other, and to him, more important, concerns.

However true this natural tendency is, the wise husband will constantly work at thoughtful signs of his love. The important thing is not that the action or gift be romantic but that it prove, in however small and practical a way, his devotion to this woman who shares his own life.

On the wife's side, she is also frequently at fault. Before marriage, she went to great expense to be attractive. She spent hours on her hair and borrowed all her sisters' dresses to be as alluring and attractive as possible. Rigid diets kept her figure under control. She learned how to be pliant and deferring, with voice always soft and melodious. In the earlier days of marriage, it is a sweet thrill for the young wife to look forward to her husband's return home from work.

How often does all this completely change, especially when children arrive on the scene. Now the husband returns home to find hardly a change in the dress of his wife or the condition of the house since he left in the morning. In devotion to her children, many a woman allows herself to drift into believing that her husband is simply "the man who came to dinner." The tender pliant woman becomes too often the demanding shrew; the warm quiet voice develops a disconcerting cutting edge.

Like her husband, it is quite natural for a woman to get lost in the multitudinous details of everyday living and to forget the end or goal for her living them. So often, in all that we do, we soon begin to see the means of achievement as the end, and the ultimate goal is forgotten.

All this does not mean that every mother must look like a blushing bride and that every household must remain in perfect order, especially after the children come. But it does mean that a loving wife will work at her attractiveness in voice and manner and try to keep her home in reasonable order. Perhaps she will not be wearing a tea gown but simply a clean and practical house dress. She will not look like she is ready to go out for the evening, but her face will be clean and sparkling and her hair combed. Perhaps she will no longer be able to feed him the choice cuts of meat, but at least the stew will be done to his taste. Perhaps the housekeeping will not be fussy, but certainly the beds will be made and the dishes washed. A smart wife will also discover how to give the children all the attention that they need while still not forgetting that her husband was there first!

The whole matter of actions which are indicative of love is not a problem of doing the same things you once did—or even doing as many things as you once did. It is a matter of habitual attention to important goals. If two people love each other as they pledged to do for a lifetime and if, in all the detailed living of every day, they are at least implicitly aware of each other, then it will be easy to achieve a delightful variety of actions which say, "I love you."

RELATIVE VALUES

Despite the "bad press" that relatives and in-laws receive in the popular imagination, most young couples starting out in wedlock discover that their relatives and in-laws can be one of their greatest assets. When you invite your relatives and dear friends to your wedding breakfast, you do not invite them merely to be present for a well-served meal and a little wedding festivity, you invite them to "second the motion" of your proposal to love each other till death parts you. They are honestly concerned that you shall make a success of your marriage and family life and they stand ready to help you in any way possible.

The support which parents and friends can give to the young couple is varied. The young husband might discover from his wife's father what makes her moody. After all, she was Daddy's girl a long time, and he should know. A bride might discover from her mother-in-law what her husband's tastes are. His mother has been cooking for him for over twenty years. The bride's mother might hurry over to rescue the bride's first dinner for the boss. It is consoling to know that, should illness strike or financial disaster threaten, a host of relatives and friends will stand by with closed ranks in encouragement and service until the crisis is past. When the first baby is due, it is good to have someone near to come in and take over for a few days. Finally, however much the interference of in-laws is feared, grandparents always seem welcome! How wonderful to have grandfather and grandmother indulge your children a little and leave their more rigid discipline to you.

Surely the young spouses should not be so childish as to use all these possible services without reason, but it is good to know that they are there. The value of relatives is particularly noticeable in their absence. The young couple who go off to set up their home in a distant place where they have neither relatives nor friends soon discover how difficult it is to start off without the active seconding of their efforts by those near and dear to them. This is one reason why there has been such rapid growth in various couples' groups throughout the country. Young couples need some sort of group support. If their business takes them into strange states, they soon find how valuable it is to band together with other couples like themselves to provide a kind of substitute family in which all the young families can become involved and concerned. When you marry, should you move to another city away from relatives and friends, be sure to search out a group such as the Christian Family Movement, Holy Family Guild, Mr. and Mrs. Clubs, etc., to find a community of interests with other families who are as interested in your family as you must be in theirs.

A few common-sense rules will help you profit from the support of parents and friends. When your husband's mother suggests that James likes his meat very rare, *listen*. Listening doesn't cost anything and might teach you a lot. After you have listened, ask her *why*. Reasons will help you understand her suggestion. When James comes home from work, *discuss* the matter with him. You might find that he really does enjoy red meat and, of course, you want to meet all his desires. On the other hand, you might discover that, long ago, he inadvertently remarked how much he enjoyed a rare steak in a restaurant. Perhaps his mother has given him rare steak ever since, and he has been afraid to tell her that he would really like it well-done. Her advice may be mistaken but it will provide an opportunity to discover the real facts of the matter.

If your wife's father advises you to invest your little nest egg in stocks or bonds, *listen*. Perhaps he does know what he is talking about. Ask him the reasons for his suggestion and, after talking it over extensively with your wife, make up your own mind. Remember that true advice is not telling someone what to do, but giving someone good reasons for making up his own mind.

As a child in a family, your first loyalties were to your parents, brothers, and sisters. Now that you are husband and wife, your first loyalty must be to each other. Scripture says, ". . . A man shall leave father and mother, and cleave to his wife, and the two shall become one flesh" (Eph. 5 : 31). A young couple will have practically no in-law problem and will gain great benefit from their relatives if they maintain their personal loyalty to each other and to their families in proper order. Gene and Joanne made this mutual loyalty very clear to their parents by a simple little strategy. They lived close to Joanne's parents and were invited each Sunday for dinner. They had no other place to go and were most happy to save their modest budget the extra expense of a large Sunday dinner. Nevertheless, each week when Joanne's mother phoned her invitation to the Sunday meal, Joanne would reply, "I don't think we are going anywhere Sunday, but I don't know what Gene's plans are. I'll talk it over with him and let you know." Each week, Joanne dutifully explained her hesitance to act without consulting Gene, and each week, for the first two years of their marriage, they gratefully partook of the parental Sunday feast. Yet she delicately and clearly made the point that, as married adults, they were free to accept or reject the invitation and were equally grateful for it.

If we examine the life of our Lord, we will discover not only how to get to heaven or become apostles, but also how to deal lovingly and effectively with relatives. Very early in His life He made it clear to His parents that He must be free to carry out His vocation. When His parents found Him in the temple and asked, "Son, why hast thou done so to us?" He answered simply, "How is it that you sought me? Did you not know that I must be about my

Father's business?" (Luke 2: 48-49). Later, at the wedding feast of Cana, He pointed out to His mother that His public ministry had not yet begun, "My hour has not yet come" (John 2: 4). When He was interrupted in His preaching with the news that His mother and relatives were outside, He made it clear that the word of God was more important, when He pointed to His audience and said, "Behold my mother and my brethren! For whoever does the will of my Father in heaven, he is my brother and sister and mother" (Matt. 12: 49-50). He even seems harsh in His defense of the mature freedom necessary for an adult Christian to meet his vocation when He says, "He who loves father or mother more than me is not worthy of me" (Matt. 10: 37). He makes it very clear to the mother of James and John (His relatives) that He will not accept interference in setting up His kingdom: ". . . as for sitting at my right hand and at my left, that is not mine to give you, but it belongs to those for whom it has been prepared by my Father" (Matt. 20: 23).

Despite Christ's declaration of independence, He does not hesitate to listen to His mother when she suggests to Him, "They have no wine" (John 2: 3). Though it is clear that His preaching mission was fully carried out in a mature fashion, careful reading of the New Testament will disclose that our Blessed Lady accompanied Her Son on most of His apostolic travels through Judea and Galilee. No doubt our Lady led many a convert to Her Son. Though our Lord preached to all the Jews and invited them all to follow Him, He does not hesitate to choose some of His apostles from among His own relatives. James and John were His cousins. Though He called His disciples to leave all and follow Him, He does not hesitate to pause and cure Peter's mother-in-law of fever. As He closed His redemptive life upon the cross, His last words included a mutual commission to His Mother and His Church (in the person of St. John) to be concerned for each other, "Woman, behold, thy son. . . . Behold, thy mother" (John 19:26, 27).

From the life of Christ, you can discover the principles upon which you can build mature independence in your vocations as husband and wife while maintaining close ties of affection, support, and respect for the respective families from which you come.

LIFE WITH MOTHER

Once a man and a woman have announced their engagement, they turn their thoughts to planning their "dream house." They begin to look for furniture and a small apartment. They might even begin to shop for a complete home. As they look through the newspapers and begin to compare costs with their tiny bank account, shock sets in. They have never realized fully how much it costs to start out "on their own."

Once they discover that their technicolor dreams have to be scaled down to grey reality, many a couple look longingly at the empty rooms in the old family homestead. They might fish eagerly for an invitation to live "just a few months with Mother." It seems very reasonable to accept such an invitation to live rent free until they can put "a few bucks in the bank." On the other hand, many parents are happy to help the young couple get started by offering them that lovely upstairs room.

Is living with Mother ever wise? It could be wise or it could be disastrous.

It could be wise to live with parents for the financial savings involved or because one or other parent is ill or aged and in need of care. Surely, children have an obligation to care for their parents, if they need care. We should not expect society in general to care for the aged. Since medical science is prolonging our lives, few young married couples can avoid the necessity of either living with their parents or of having their parents eventually come to live with them at some future date. With our modern longevity, to pretend that your parents can live independently of you until death is rather unrealistic.

On the other hand, "living with Mother" can be disastrous. You are no longer children and you want to live a fully adult life. Yet it is extremely difficult for parents to realize that you now have reached adult status and are able to make decisions on your own. For years they told you what to do and expected complete obedience. It will be quite difficult for them to abdicate their parental function and live with you on an adult level. They are so concerned for your happiness that it will be extremely difficult for them to keep "hands off." Only if you are able to come to decisions without running to Mother for approval and only if your parents are able to resist any temptation to overpossessiveness will living in the old family homestead work.

Some advisors suggest that, should you wish to live at home for the first few months, you agree on a definite amount of time and then leave when that time is up. Otherwise you will discover that the six months becomes a year, and a year two or three years, while you give the impression of sponging upon parental generosity. This can only bring resentment on their side and guilty feelings on yours. Other advisors suggest that you should live apart from your parents, for the first few months of marriage at least. They suggest that this will give you an opportunity really to adapt to each other and make your first marital adjustments without any sense of being observed, criticized, or pressured. Should financial pressures or parental need suggest that you return home, you can return, not as children, but as adults who have proved your declaration of independence and ability to live apart.

Whether you decide to start your marriage living with either set of parents, or perhaps return to live with them at a later date, remember that it is their home. They have spent years fixing up the house, buying the furniture they like, developing their own color schemes, and setting up their own customs. Quite naturally, you want to live your own life, and you would like to move in and change everything. After years of experimentation, Mother and Dad have set up a routine for meal hours, attendance at Sunday Mass, division of labor, and even schedules for the use of the bathroom! Be content to fit in with their program. Perhaps even your desire to entertain friends will have to be curtailed because your parents, poor old-timers, like to go to bed early.

If you move in with Mother, contribute to the welfare of the household. Insist on bearing some share of the expenses, even if your parents oppose this. You will have the conviction that you are not a parasite and you will preclude any growing resentment that you are taking their help for granted. A more important contribution than money is work. Don't expect your parents to treat you as hotel guests who simply take the conveniences of living for granted. As a young wife you will want to pitch in with the dishes, cooking, bed-making, dusting, laundry and cleaning. As a young husband, you should certainly expect to lend your youthful muscles to household repairs, painting, lifting, etc.

There is a lot of truth to the saying, "No kitchen is big enough for two women." Even though your mother trained you fully to do housework and to cook, you still like to develop your own techniques as wife and mother. There will be endless friction if you try to do the same tasks together. It is much better to divide up the household work so that mother and daughter do different tasks or rotate the tasks between them. Clean upstairs while Mother cleans downstairs. If possible, let Mother cook Monday's evening meal while you take Tuesday's and Thursday's. This should keep you from "getting into each other's hair."

Above all, the young couple who live with their parents need adequate privacy. They should have a room with a solidly closing door to which they can retire to be alone. Why? You are romantically in love. You want to use all the pet names you discovered during courtship; you want to kiss and embrace. In short, you want to act out the sweet madness which is romantic love. The "old folks" may make you feel quite embarrassed. They might even suggest that this is all quite silly and unrealistic, and it is about time you settled down. Perhaps they could be even a bit envious that their love no longer has the "zing" that yours exhibits. They might even bitterly suggest that you are silly and unrealistic, or worse, they might poke fun at you. You need real privacy, free from observation and eavesdropping, to be really in love.

You need privacy not only for the expression of love, but also to express those early disagreements and even angers or frustrations which may develop. After all, this early portion of marriage is your "shake-down cruise," and things rarely run with perfect smoothness in the beginning. It is hard to carry on an argument in whispers. It is equally impossible to solve a dispute in a burst of tears, mutual apologies, or amorous love when you are performing in front of an audience.

During courtship, a future husband and wife should find many hours to talk out the possibilities and probabilities of living with parents. No possible solution should simply be taken for granted. It is utterly unfair for one partner to plan to live in the parental mansion while the other partner discovers the plan only after having irrevocably committed himself by saying, "I do."

Chapter Ten

MARRIAGE AND MONEY

MANAGING THE MONEY

The best answer I have ever heard to a pugnacious question, "Who manages the money in your house?" was the answer, "What money?" Most arguments along this line flow from selfish fear that one or the other partner will be put upon or will lose his integrity as a free human adult. Most of the money which comes into the normal American home is spent before it arrives simply by the fact that there are fixed expenses to living, upon which the couple have agreed from the early days of their marriage. Rent or mortgage money does not need managing, it needs only paying. Fixed expenses like time-payments, telephone, water, electric and gas bills need very little money management. To a large extent even food bills cannot be managed too finely. Three growing children will need a certain number of quarts of milk a day and very little management can be exercised to cut down the bill.

When it comes to paying the fixed bills or involving the family in any regular expenditure, certainly both partners are involved and each should consult the other. Someone has said that the woman doesn't mind at all being the junior partner in the firm but she does want to belong to it. Every major expense, every involvement of future income, every savings plan should be given a great deal of thought and discussion between husband and wife. Neither is a minor depending on a decision of a guardian!

When it comes to actually paying the bills, who makes out the checks is obviously unimportant. But when it comes to managing money in such a way that the maximum is achieved in areas where fixed expenses are not involved, then the young couple must find their own pattern. Some men discover that they simply cannot keep to a budget, that they hardly know where the money has gone. They discover further that their blissful confidence in their ability to provide for their families leads them to foolish impulse buying. Such a husband who finds the hole in all his pockets, should not hesitate to hand over detailed management to his wife. In doing so he does not abdicate his masculinity, he merely faces facts. Still, if he is wise, he retains for himself the position of "chairman of the board." On the other hand, it sometimes happens that a young wife discovers that she is the naturally extravagant and improvident member of the family. She discovers at the end of the week that the food budget is gone and there is no food in the house. She should, of course, set about learning the skills which will teach her wise buying and she can well ask her husband to help her reach the weekend with a balanced budget and a balanced refrigerator.

Sometimes married couples—and I suspect this applies to most—find it easier to divide up the responsibility between them. In such families a husband usually takes over investments, savings, housing, taxes, major improvements, etc., whereas he hands over to his wife the detailed spending for clothing, food, and daily household needs. Such a plan seems eminently practical today, when a man is forced to be so much away from home and his wife must do the purchasing of daily items. It also is valuable in giving to each member an area of responsible adulthood in money matters. Of course, it implies that neither will involve the family in a major expense without consultation with the other.

Whatever method of money management is used by the couple, there should always be some small amount assigned to each of them to spend as they wish. Some husbands and wives call this "cigarette money" even when neither smokes. A few dollars a week to be spent, at whim if so desired, gives a tremendous sense of freedom. The wife might like to buy little personal items whose purchase might make her feel guilty if she took them from the family budget; the husband might like a little penny-ante poker. Either might like to save up a small amount over a period of time and surprise the other with an unexpected gift. One partner might simply wish to let it sit and grow. One might want to cover up errors in the standard budget from this little sinking fund. It makes little difference what is done with this small amount; the important thing is that a small area of freedom (almost of irresponsibility!) gives a sense of lightness to everyday living.

Whether money management is divided or handled more directly by one or the other, an imperative family quality in handling money is honesty. Every new skill involves mistakes and errors. The young bride may discover that she has yielded to the pressure of a door salesman to buy a vacuum cleaner they neither can afford nor need. It will be better for her to admit her mistake immediately and try to remedy it with the help of her husband than to try covering it up. If nothing else is accomplished, it will at least save the emotional wear and tear of constant anxiety lest the indiscretion be discovered. The young husband may have made a foolish investment while his wife blissfully believes that things are going smoothly. Unless he tells her, she may begin to think he is niggardly and unsympathetic when he steers the conversation away from the needed living-room suite. On his side, he can hope for encouragement to recoup the loss and will then lose the tremendous sense of urgency to have his ship come in, which might lead him into even more foolish gambles. All this is similar to those practical youngsters who prefer to admit a fault and be punished immediately than hide it and live in fear.

When two people become spouses, they attempt to become two-in-one-flesh. They thereby become one principle of generation. When they unite all their abilities, they try to become one principle of action, one source of joy, one economic unit. Teamwork is, therefore, the answer in money management. There is no reason to agree with the youngster who defines a budget as "a family quarrel." Working together toward economic security and prudent management is but one further area of possible delight in unity.

SPENDING THE MONEY

Much disunity in marriage could be prevented if men and women could understand that their characteristic approaches to financial matters are quite different. A man tends to look upon money as a value in itself. If he can look upon the black numbers in his bank book and find them satisfactory, he can sit back and point to himself as a successful man. If he has enough greenbacks to buy things, he might invest in a Cadillac, a summer home, or a yacht, not because he wishes to use them but because they simply seem worthwhile to own. If he is a wage-earner and comes home exhausted at the end of his work week, he banks his check or gives it to his wife and begs her, "Please hang onto it. I'm tired. I've succeeded in keeping the roof over our heads, food in our stomaches for another week. See how far you can make it stretch."

A woman, however, has another approach entirely. To a woman money is not an end or goal in itself, it is a means to surround her loved ones with comfort. A woman sees money as a mere medium of exchange for the values which are never good enough to satisfy her longing to coddle her loved ones. This does not mean that a woman is naturally improvident or that money in the bank does not mean security to her, but it will always remain an enigma to her that money must remain unused in a bank when it could be put to work so wonderfully in her home.

Even in their attitude toward saving, men and women are different. When a man does without something in order to save, or buys a less expensive item than the more expensive one he would like to have, he salts the saving away. On the other hand, when a woman saves, she spends! The pennies she has saved by careful shopping and persual of sales advertisements, she now feels free to put into another expenditure. And to her, this is true saving because she has used her money to the wisest possible extent and obtained more things for the same amount of money.

Another difference between the sexes in their approach to economics is exemplified by this statement: "A man will spend two dollars for a one-dollar item he is convinced he needs. A woman will spend one dollar for a two-dollar item she does not need at all." Once a wife convinces her husband that something is necessary for him or the home, he will gladly buy it immediately, regardless of its cost, and even if it demands that he carry a debt; but he will complain that he sees no necessity for endless shopping since, after all, "that costs shoe leather." He will frequently ignore quality (particularly in clothing) simply because he needs an item at this time and sees no reason for doing without it. On the other hand, in her natural desire to stretch her dollar to buy two things, a woman sometimes finds it difficult to avoid foolish expenses simply because she cannot bear to let the bargain go by.

If each will use the strength of the other, expenses will be wisely incurred. The woman will do well to pause if her husband is not convinced that an expenditure is necessary. On the other hand, she will be freed of much anxiety at what seems to her a dangerous indebtedness if he is willing to risk and to work for a necessary item. A man will do well, on the other side, to allow his wife her almost inborn ability to shop wisely. Since she is not being paid on an hourly basis, the hours she spends saving a penny here, a penny there (though seemingly inefficient from a masculine point of view) will nevertheless stretch family income beyond his fondest dreams. If a woman will become wise enough to keep a list of family needs and wait for the special sales, she can give full rein to her appetite to spend one dollar for a two-dollar item, so long as she sticks to her list.

Finally, though men may be generally better at mathematics than women, wives seem to know much more clearly where every penny has gone. Most men would find themselves hard put to tell anyone where their spending money has gone for a week. Most wives can tell you each penny, even if they cannot balance the books!

The different approaches of men and women to economics should not be a source of disunity and misunderstanding but a source of mutual aid. If each will promote the strength of the other and each will allow his or her weaknesses to be supplied by those strengths, material goods will not be a rock on which the marriage will be split but one upon which it will be founded. The subtle reality which can be achieved is well illustrated in the little story of the man who gazed wistfully and enviously upon a visiting friend and family who were leaving in their new Cadillac. He turned to his wife and, with some courage and fire still in his eyes, said, "Someday, dear, we, too, will be rich." His wife smiled quietly and confidently and said, "Dear, we are rich. Someday we will have money." With this kind of ambition wedded to this kind of clear-headed vision and encouragement, a young couple can face calmly the future and its uncertainties.

HAPPINESS AND MONEY

An elderly couple once told a young couple that "Two people can get along on practically nothing if the neighbors and in-laws could be content to get along with less than nothing." Another couple suggested that "It is not so much that you must be satisfied with what you have, but you must also be satisfied with what your neighbor has!" The final clarification came when a wise couple suggested, "The whole problem of money is learning to adjust your net income to your *gross* habits." All of which advice suggests that we must learn to be content with what we can reasonably have.

Very seldom does the amount of money make any difference to the happiness of the young couple, unless they disagree on what they have or should have. Friction is caused not so much from not having an extra five dollar bill as from disagreeing about what to do with it when you have it. A man might want to put his five dollars into the bank or into the family car; a woman will tend to put her five dollars into new curtains for the kitchen.

There is no doubt that fundamental needs must be met. The young couple who blissfully spend on recreation the money which is needed to keep a roof over their heads, clothing on their bodies, and food in their stomachs, will soon find themselves in sore straits. They cannot continue to live without fundamental food, clothing, and shelter.

Once fundamental needs have been taken care of, the couple can begin to look around them for conveniences and luxuries. It is quite possible to cook a meal on a simple four-burner gas stove, but it is more convenient to have the push-button type. It is quite possible to do laundry in a conventional washing machine and hang your clothes out on the line, but it is more convenient to have an automatic washer-dryer combination. It is quite possible to go to and from work by streetcar or bus, but it might be more convenient to own and operate a car. The problem arises when conveniences become near-necessities. After all, conveniences can be indefinitely extended and then the tail begins to wag the dog. Families where the breadwinner has lost his job due to a recession, frequently refuse to give up their phone or fancy television set because they have lost their perspective of the necessary and useful. By all means, the young couple should acquire conveniences as they go through life, but they should not hope to start their married life with every possible convenience, nor can they ever safely lose their perspective. Some couples foolishly start out their married lives with a brand new car upon which they will spend four or five thousand dollars over a period of three years in cost and maintenance and discover to their sorrow that they have nothing to show for this investment. It would probably be better for their health and happiness if they had walked for the first three years!

Every young couple needs some recreation. Recreation does not necessarily demand expensive dinners, nightclubs and theatre tickets, but it does demand some place within the budget. Sometimes a young couple, determined to make a fine economic start in marriage, will try to find their recreation only in each other. This is disastrous, since God made not only work but also play. On the other hand, many modern couples feel that they are only truly living when they are having fun. Daily work gives them no satisfaction or sense of accomplishment and they live only for their weekends and evenings. This is as dangerous as the opposite position. Recreation means just what it says: it is a re-creation, a making new; it is letting the clock-spring wind down so that it may be again wound up; it is relaxing the strings of the violin so that they will not snap when tuned. The important thing to remember, however, is that the clock must be wound in order to run and the strings must be in tension in order to be in tune!

What is considered necessary, convenient, or recreational for a given couple must be decided between themselves. Some couples will seem to need more living space than others. The convenience of, say, a dish-washer will be more important to one couple whereas an automatic dryer will seem more important to another. One couple may find four movies a month each followed by a trip to the local hamburger stand the best possible recreation whereas another couple might prefer a rare dinner out followed by an expensive theatre performance. It is not important that you spend your income in the way others spend it; it is only important that you set up your own system of values *together*. The young Christian husband and wife will find budgeting problems remarkably simplified if they maintain a Christian approach to material possessions. Some people are convinced that the world owes them a living and that their need to work is only a necessary evil, a wall which keeps them from what they ought to have by right. Others feel that material possessions are the sign of success and the guarantee of happiness in this life. Still others make of material things a god. Finally, some Christians feel that, if possible, they should actually reject material things and pursue only the devotion to God.

All of these positions are more or less wrong. The true Christian accepts reverently the material world about him as the gift of God upon which he is to work in order to transform it and make it truly serviceable to himself and his neighbors on their road to heaven. A Christian works willingly to render some service to the community from which he can obtain a just return. He refuses to make material goods his only values. He maintains a detachment from them which permits him to be happy whether he has them or not. Yet, on the other hand, he does not despise the gifts of God and works hard to build those reasonable financial comforts and securities which, as Pope Pius XI said, are not hazardous to, but conducive towards Christian life. With a good Christian attitude towards material things, money management and marriage will go easily together.